New Hotel Design

Otto Riewoldt

New Hotel Design

Otto Riewoldt

Watson-Guptill Publications

Published in the United States in 2002 by Watson-Guptill Publications,
a division of VNU Business Media, Inc.,
770 Broadway, New York, N.Y. 10003
www.watsonguptill.com

Library of Congress Catalog Card Number: 2001097324

ISBN: 0-8230-2339-7

Published in the United Kingdom in 2002 by
Laurence King Publishing Ltd.
71 Great Russell Street
London WC1B 3BP

Designed by Price Watkins
Printed in Hong Kong

First printing, 2002
1 2 3 4 5 6 7 8 9 / 10 09 08 07 06 05 04 03 02

Frontispiece: reception desk of The Standard hotel, Los Angeles

The author would like to thank Price Watkins for their elegant
design of the book; Simon Cowell for his kind and patient co-operation
in editing this book; all the architects and designers whose work
has been reproduced; and the various hotels and corporations that
supplied additional information on the projects featured.

contents

introduction

'He was dazed from lack of sleep, and everything had the dramatic, believably fantastic quality of a dream. Suddenly from the room above him he heard the rhythmic movements of lovemaking. He listened – at first it was as if the bed were breathing . . . and then it seemed like the panting of a thief on the run.'

William Goyen, *Ghost and Flesh*, 1952

The sensuous aesthetics of contemporary hotel design

MODERN hotel design is responsible for more bold, colourful and imaginative creations than any other architectural genre. Never before has there been such amazing diversity, such a potpourri of styles or such extravagant playfulness. Today's hotel scene is like a box of chocolates – full of delightful confections, which present business travellers and holidaymakers alike with deliciously agonizing choices.

Taste is highly subjective, of course, and money is as instrumental as ever in defining exclusivity. Price and brand glamour still matter, but don't necessarily eclipse connoisseurship. Today's sophisticated and trend-conscious hotel guests take pleasure from savouring the very latest discoveries ahead of the crowd – in hotels just as much as in the worlds of art and fashion.

The latest developments in hotel design, as described in this book, reflect four main themes: ascetic modernism, nostalgic opulence, extravagant fantasy and exotic exclusivity. Drawing on these themes, chains and individual hotels adopt individual design strategies to enhance their brand images in an increasingly global marketplace. Three trends are predominant. First, quality has markedly improved in the business hotel sector, where the self-referential interiors of the designer hotels have been softened and skilfully reinterpreted with an emphasis on comfort. Second, both designer hotels and business hotels are making a significant contribution to urban regeneration. In London, for example, commercial buildings in the West End have been transformed into brilliantly original hotels (including One Aldwych and Philippe Starck's first two European projects, St Martin's Lane and the Sanderson), while ailing but venerable railway hotels, such as the Great Eastern at Liverpool Street station and the Great Western at Paddington, are given modern makeovers. Third, hotel design is embracing the opportunies offered by ethno-cultural diversity. Several years ago, the South-east Asian Armanpuri group came up with the idea of incorporating local styles and cultural traditions into luxury hideaways; now even the larger chains such as Four Seasons and Oberoi are moving confidently into this expanding upmarket sector.

The two main, contrasting forces in modern hotel design are the 'intensive' strategy, which focuses on small, expensive hotels where guests can expect the very highest quality of facilities and services (as found in the rejuvenated, lavishly redecorated Grand Hotels), and the 'extensive' strategy, whereby ever larger and more lavish self-contained leisure utopias are conjured up everywhere from Las Vegas to Dubai.

Quite apart from their design attributes, today's hotels have to fulfil two key requirements as the temporary homes of business travellers: they must function effectively as fully networked workplaces and they must offer a wide range of relaxation possibilities. Rooms offering internet access and other communications facilities have become commonplace in such hotels; business centres are vital to ensure that the nomads of the information age have access to office equipment wherever and whenever they need it.

Installing digital facilities does not generally have much impact on a hotel's basic architectural structure, but the same cannot be said about the luxury facilities for sports and relaxation – often designed with a touch of exoticism – that are becoming a standard feature of many city hotels. Wherever their work may take them, today's business executives and professionals want to be pampered in every way. Health consciousness is increasing, and the modern concept of 'wellness' has less to do with rock-hard muscles than with physical and psychological contentedness. The American term 'spa' – supposedly derived from the Latin *salus per aqua* (well-being through water) – is frequently used for these oases of physical indulgence; within hotels they are often operated as spatially integrated but economically independent units open to the wider public as well as to hotel guests.

The power of images

A PROPER analysis of new developments in hotel design must go beyond the superficial world of stylistic vocabularies, design trends and conceptual strategies. The contemporary aesthetic can only be understood against a backdrop of the fundamental changes taking place in architecture, tourism and consumer perceptions.

An important issue here is the power of images. Our understanding of reality is increasingly conditioned by a fascination – or even a fixation – with the mythologies of the entertainment industry. These clichés define and limit our imaginative powers: we look for experiences in the real world that correspond to the illusions created by film, television and advertisements. Media manipulation of fantasy and perception is the source of an economically driven process, identified by the film director Martin Scorsese as 'Disneyfication'. The saturation of our senses with prefabricated images of what is desirable and pleasurable is progressing apace: leisure is becoming synonymous with entertainment, and entertainment value is the key to consumer behaviour.

It is all about turning life into a theme park. It is about idealized worlds that supposedly can be made real, worlds with a high 'recognition value'; it is also about instant gratification. The epidemic that started decades ago in amusement parks has long since taken hold in retail environments, restaurants and hotels. Today the competition to engage customers' attention and emotions means – above all – a competition for their time. The aim is to ensnare us in a unique world that is alternately familiar and surprising.

If today's theme parks are, in the words of the Italian writer Umberto Eco, 'allegories of consumer society', then 'experience' hotels embody its creative desires – the material counterparts, both subtle and striking in their effects, of changes in behaviour and expectations. A hotel stay is almost always a transitory experience – giving the sense of a life dipped into – and this fact has shaped the hotel as a genre. Where else can the philosophy expressed by the German baroque poet Andreas Gryphius – 'we are but guests on the earth, restlessly wandering' – be experienced more elementally? Where else can personal identity be changed more freely and with less inhibition, albeit for a short time? In a hotel anyone can pretend to be different from what he or she is in ordinary life. 'No one is concerned with others in a big hotel. Everyone is alone with themselves. Perhaps at night someone steals from their room into someone else's room – but that's all. Behind this lies a profound isolation. In their room, everyone is alone with their ego and no "you" can be reached or held.' Despite its pessimistic tone, Vicky Baum's observation in her novel *Hotel Shanghai* holds out the promise of a liberation from self through anonymous individuality.

'In a hotel, guests should find what they dream of at home,' said Conrad Hilton, one of the founders of the modern hotel industry. 'Experience' hotels aim to live up to this aspiration, whether the concept is based on a dream of Hollywood or the work of a star designer. In a highly targeted way visitors are given a surface onto which they can project their fantasies and obsessions. The hotel becomes a stage, a film set, a place where guests can enact their desires and learn more about themselves. The escapism is effective because the opportunity to change roles, to act out a usually hidden side of oneself, follows a predefined formula. The expedition into semi-private worlds of secret desires and barely suppressed illusions begins with the choice of story and setting. The spaces and props for enacting the ritual are drawn from the stylistic repertoires of classicism, kitsch and avant-garde.

It is no coincidence that the leading representative of this transformation in hotel design is the French designer Philippe Starck. He was the first in the late 1980s to treat his interiors as stage sets, to assemble them using quotations and surprises, to arrange them as stimulating scene changes that are playfully managed and discovered by the guests; and he has done this in increasingly virtuoso fashion ever since. In doing this he anticipated the needs and desires of the consumer élite of the information age.

The American sociologist David Brooks recently coined the term 'bourgeois bohemians' (or 'bobos') to describe this élite. The bobos have grown up with multimedia literacy, style-consciousness and self-awareness. For them, durability is just as important as curiosity value – their quest is for quality in all things, as they alternate between power-working and serious relaxation. The combination of efficiency and hedonism in their lives, of Protestant work ethic and Dionysian self-indulgence, gives rise to what might be called a gentle materialism – and they react to images and new experiences in a correspondingly light-hearted and self-confident manner. They behave as consumers in the same way as they surf the net, and they check into a hotel in the same way as they check into their other life situations – on a temporary basis.

Architecture as visual sensation

EMOTIONAL qualities, powerful images and unmediated expressiveness are the most prominent elements of contemporary architecture. Buildings are designed as adventures for the senses: overpowering, imperious, entertaining. 'We are much more concerned with creating a building that arouses emotions, rather than one that represents this or that idea,' explains the Swiss architect Jacques Herzog. His Dutch colleagues Ben van Berkel and Caroline Bos identify the main features of an architecture of sensation; it should be 'anticipatory, unexpected, climactic, cinematic, time-related, non-linear, surprising, mysterious, compelling and engaging'.

Integral to the very nature of architecture and interior design is an artificial world of experience, but the creation of visual sensations and spatial illusions was for a long time subordinate to artistic, psychological and economic concerns. In 1947, in the book *Vision in Motion*, Bauhaus artist Laszlo Moholy-Nagy asserted that artworks and buildings should be seen as constructed sensual experiences, and that it is the artist's task 'to put layer upon layer, stone upon stone, in the organization of emotions; to record feeling with his particular means, to give structure and refinement as well as direction to the inner life of his contemporaries'.

Modern architecture can be read as the fulfilment of this injunction. On one hand it creates one-offs with no general relevance — buildings that, like modernist works of art, stand alone; on the other hand it creates theatrical décors made up of quotations or borrowings from popular culture. In both cases it is moving away from the representation of functions and from architectural typology towards autonomy, excess, nostalgia and spectacle. The 'wow!' factor is what counts.

The result is an architecture of grand gestures and big names. It is not political or religious power or the representation of community that lies behind the attention-grabbing, monumental constructions of today. These are the cathedrals of the leisure culture — museums and arts complexes, airports, mega-malls, hybrid mixed-use complexes, hotel-casino resorts — which seem to lay claim to an exalted status purely on the basis of their size. Popular culture has turned architecture into a brand logo; architectural design is entertainment 'capital' used in a targeted way by investors, politicians and brand strategists as a magnet for the public and a marketing instrument and, above all, as a source of profit.

The French writer Michel Houellebecq sums it up as follows: 'Contemporary architecture implicitly takes on a simple agenda: it builds the shelves of society's supermarket. The logic of the supermarket necessarily leads to a dispersal of desire. And this superficial, shallow participation in the life of the world is designed to replace the longing for existence.' According to Houellebecq, if 'modern architecture is no longer called upon' to 'build places to live in', then it will come to see itself as an inventor of environments for passers-by, visitors and travellers, and of consumer attractions.

Architects are in demand as suppliers of spectacle. Event architecture — opening up the city as an arena for events — is made possible only by what the German architect Axel Schultes criticized as the 'architectural audacities of egomaniacs'. The Bauhaus ideal of the democratization of the arts becomes the vulgarization of style. Supposedly distinctive architectural images are increasingly interchangeable. A key characteristic here is architecture's detachment from its context. The invasion of the human imagination by the myths of the entertainment industry has led to a proliferation of globally compatible architectural monuments that bear no relation at all to their surroundings.

The validity of philosopher Jean Paul Baudrillard's thesis of 'architecture's disappearance into the virtual', where 'reality turns into spectacle, the real becomes a theme park' is now apparent. In Las Vegas, the booming US leisure metropolis in the Nevada desert, counterfeits are piled up to the point where they become overpowering realities. For the American architects Denise Scott-Brown and Robert Venturi, who wrote the book *Learning from Las Vegas* more than three decades ago, a decisive change has since taken place: the change 'from symbol to scenario', from iconography to scenography, in which the New York skyline, the Eiffel Tower and Venice's St Mark's Square are set, chaotically and confusingly, side by side. An amusement-driven world theatre has left the auditorium to evolve into an open-air parade of curiosities. The city itself has become a cliché-laden interior; the architecture works with suggestive strategies and foreshortened perspectives, more or less turning itself into a three-dimensional stage backdrop.

To use a term coined by Robert E. Somol, professor of architecture in Los Angeles, this 'architainment landscape' is based on a universal architectural model: the hotel-casino with attached shopping, show, conference and trade-fair facilities. Here, Endo urbanism – the transplantation and accumulation of set pieces – is inverted in the stage-set hotel, in its simulated privacy, where the strange attracts by means of the familiar. These environments for sale are temporary homes offering timebound attractions.

In the 1920s the Viennese novelist Joseph Roth described a situation that still applies to most of the thousands of hotel rooms piled on top of one another in Las Vegas: 'In this room, fortunately, there is nothing, not a single item, that the eye would linger on with grief. When my suitcases are taken away, others will stand here. When I no longer stand at this window, others will stand here. This room creates no illusions – for itself, for you, for me. When I leave it and look back at it, it is no longer my room. The day is long, for there is no melancholy to fill it with.' The difference is that today, beyond the simple accommodation, a multitude of temptations, targeted on the senses and the wallet, awaits the traveller – all the consumer attractions in the world absorbed into a garish adventure playground for the whole family, where the only compulsion to linger is the promise of unadulterated pleasure.

It may seem that a vast chasm separates the rowdy world of Las Vegas from the subtle décors of the purist designer hotels, but the mega-palaces of kitsch and the small temples of contemporary style both offer 'mood' architecture, carefully devised backdrops against which guests can enjoy new experiences. In this they follow the rules of the 'experience economy' analysed by the authors B. Joseph Pine II and James H. Gilmore, which operates in a highly manipulative way: 'Theatre is not a metaphor but a model. Staging experiences is not about entertaining customers, it's about engaging them.' Ian Schrager, who remains a trendsetter in the élite sector with his Starck hotels, compares the hotel's spatial layout with a play: the lobby is the prelude, the first act of the hotel's drama, which has its finale in the individual guest rooms. In recent projects such as London's St Martin's Lane, guests can even influence their own happy ending by adjusting the stage lighting in their rooms to the colours they desire.

Interiors are planned to the last detail. Restaurants, signs, graphic designs and the appearance of the hotel personnel have to meet, in a clear and consistent way, the expectations of a cosmopolitan public well versed in the language of fashion and advertising. 'They were the messengers of the Lord, selected for their upright stature and attractive faces – advantages that were amply exhibited in their carriage and the look in their eyes. They were angels of this world.' This is how, in the 1930s, the German writer Wolfgang Koeppen saw the reception staff in the parallel and more beautiful universe that a hotel represents. To bring his vision up to date, the only thing you would have to add would be the name of the exclusive designer or brand responsible for creating the angels' uniforms.

'Image transfer' is an increasingly important concept in both the popular and élite sectors of the hotel business. Leading figures in modern architecture such as the Dutch architect Rem Koolhaas and the Swiss duo Jacques Herzog and Pierre de Meuron have been engaged by the fashion company Prada to design its new flagship stores and headquarters – the hotelier Ian Schrager invited the same stars to design the Astor Palace in New York's SoHo, the first new-build hotel in his luxury chain, before he changed his mind and transfered the project to the even more illustruous Frank O. Gehry. Schrager's local competitor André Balasz responded by having his latest hotel project, the Broadway – just a few blocks away – designed by Jean Nouvel. The battle for customers' attention is fought between star architects in Manhattan in just the same way as it is fought between gigantic postcard panoramas of fictional and non-fictional sites.

The booming 'experience' economy

IN the fiercely competitive market place of global tourism, money is more important than style. In the untroubled times before the September 11 terrorist attacks in New York and Washington DC, regions and cities anywhere in the world can get themselves on the holiday map within a few years by making huge investments in tourism. The best example is Dubai in the United Arab Emirates, which has established a place for itself in the luxury market sector at enormous expense, thereby securing a degree of independence from declining oil revenues. Even such a traditional millionaires' hideaway as Monte Carlo is embarking on a lavish development programme with the aim of attracting affluent young gamblers with families as well as its more mature clientele.

Disneyland Paris has more than twice as many visitors as the Louvre; the Las Vegas counterfeit The Venetian has more rooms than all the hotels in the real Venice combined; and Las Vegas itself outstrips both New

York and Paris in terms of overall hotel capacity. The figures speak for themselves: the boom in the 'experience' economy, characterized by artificially confected entertainment packages, is the engine driving the global boom in tourism. The hotel business is a highly profitable component of the tourist 'value creation' chain, and vertically integrated travel groups are becoming ever more heavily involved in this sector.

At the same time, mid-market hotels are coming under pressure. The budget sector is recording steady growth rates, although the highest rates of growth are in the four- and five-star sector. Major national and international hotel chains are responding to increasing diversification by developing strategies to target particular customer groups. For example, Marriott International, based in Atlanta, USA, is marketing its total of nearly 400,000 beds worldwide under 12 different brands. Former national chains are expanding into international markets, while international chains are consolidating their global presence. The Singapore-based Raffles Group is opening a new luxury hotel in Berlin, and the French group Sofitel is opening one in Chicago. At the same time the economic life of hotels is getting shorter: hotel projects are now planned over amortization periods of only 10 to 15 years; there is an increasing demand for the new.

Investors now decide on a particular designer or style at a very early stage in the development of a hotel, and operators have to live with these choices when they are supplied with completely fitted turnkey hotels – as was the case with the Ritz-Carlton in Wolfsburg and the Grand Hyatt in Berlin. Such a separation between the operational business and the design process remains an exception, however. In large-scale mixed-use projects the hotel increasingly performs an anchor role. A hotel in a commercial mall is designed as a prime public attraction, drawing in not only hotel guests but also the general public. In the heart of Berlin, a former communist hotel block was demolished to make way for the new 'DomAquarée', where a 30m high cylindrical saltwater aquarium, big enough for sharks and rays, will be a permanent attraction in the atrium of the new Radisson hotel (scheduled to open in 2003). The two-storey lift taking guests up to the health centre on the top floor 'floats' right through the aquarium. Generally, restaurants and shopping areas are becoming ever more important elements in a hotel complex, making the hotel a focal point in the urban environment and a place where local folk can meet and socialize. Single-use buildings – used purely for accommodation or conferences – are a thing of the past.

A current trend in the world of hotel design is the replication of a successful formula. Ian Schrager's 'one-offs' are opening at an ever faster rate – the existing establishments currently have a combined total of 5400 beds and seven new hotels will be added by 2002, including the St Moritz in New York (in addition to the Astor Palace mentioned above), the Clifton in San Francisco and the Miramar in Santa Barbara. 'I think the market is infinite because it's about stimulation, subversion, freshness,' says Schrager. Dirk Gädeke, the founder of the European Art'otels Group, is clearly thinking along similar lines. He is planning 40 new art hotels under a franchising arrangement in collaboration with the Park Plaza chain.

The trend is evident in everything from original designs to brand image. The Dorint Group of Germany, once very conservative in style, has repositioned itself further upmarket by opening city hotels with an emphasis on design. W Suites, the design hotel subsidiary of the world's largest hotel group, Starwood – which also includes Westin and the St Regis luxury group, among others – continues to consolidate its position in the USA and is planning a move into international markets. A series of new 'style hotels' is planned to rejuvenate the portfolio of the UK's Hilton group – starting with the Trafalgar hotel in London. Smaller chains, such as the UK's Firmdale Hotels or California's Joie de Vivre group, are successfully serving a more offbeat customer base. The booking and marketing group Design Hotels is flourishing, too, with more than 100 hotels currently under its wing. The 'boutique hotel' (more compact and individual in its design than average), which has long been the province of the avant-garde, is now recognized as a successful model for small luxury hotels, in urban and rural settings.

Another aspect of the replication strategy – whether it applies to groups or to individual hotels – is the drive to develop a cohesive brand image and extend this image to include the hotel's furnishings and fittings. Merchandizing outlets – where guests can buy or order furniture and accessories – are not so much a symptom of today's trivia culture as a welcome additional source of revenue for top hotels from Ritz-Carlton through to the Schrager group. The idea of translating the splendour of the Gleneagles hotel in Scotland into a new luxury brand for upmarket consumer goods may have been abandoned, but parts of the concept were used in the renovation of this high-class establishment.

The upmarket hotel sector has attracted top names in the fashion world, some of whom have followed successful licensing deals for perfumes and cosmetics with a leap into interior design collections, making hotels the logical next step. Versace, Ferragamo and Bulgari have launched joint ventures with groups such as Marriott and Kempinski. At the popular end of the spectrum, global consumer brands are waking up to the potential of hotels: in 2001 the fast food giant McDonald's opened its first hotel in Zurich; famous names in the 'experience' restaurant trade such as Hard Rock Cafe and House of Blues are already active in the hotel sphere.

Although the economic fallout of the September 11 terrorist attacks has cast even darker clouds over the international tourist trade than over other industries, the general upward trend is still unbroken. Bookings and occupancies are temporarily affected, investments postponed, but there are already signs of recovery.

The authenticity of illusion

HUMAN beings create their own images of desire and then set out in pursuit of them. These are simulacra: ideals, visions, idols. Pilgrims and travellers have a great deal in common, and unspoiled nature serves merely as a backdrop for the experiences we thirst after. The denunciation of tourism is as old as organized mass travel itself. When the poet William Wordsworth vehemently attacked the construction of a railway line serving his beloved Lake District in 1844, he was reacting to the consequences of his own romantic vision of the place, which had made it an attraction for nature-hungry city dwellers.

Since then the tourist industry has been a driving force in consumer society and at the same time a symbol of its self-destructive powers. Even a representative of the architectural avant-garde such as Elia Zenghelis acknowledges this paradox: 'The tourists' invasion violates the "purity" of this culture, which the traveller searches for in vain. Their arrival has a devastating impact in the locality and their departure leaves ineffable melancholy and desolation.' Travel as a luxury item was democratized through mass modes of transport – first the train, then the aeroplane – but the relentless process of social levelling has turned global diversity into a colourful picture-postcard landscape, all the more so in the post-industrial age. The fate of Campione on Lake Garda illustrates the way things are going: the village once housed workers from the local cotton-spinning mill (long since closed down); now Cartier boss Dominique Perrin plans to transform it into a peaceful, exclusive holiday hideaway for the idle rich.

Yet perhaps simulation itself becomes authentic when it overlies the inherited reality, annexes it and simultaneously becomes a point of reference in itself. There is no doubt that Las Vegas and Disney World have attained the status of originals – originals that others quote and imitate. For the American art critic David Hickey, Las Vegas is even 'the only authentic image world on the North American continent'. In Las Vegas, artificial worlds are adorned with genuine artistic masterpieces and original architecture. Behind the glittering façades on the imitation Lake Como shirt-sleeved visitors to Hotel Bellagio can see works by Picasso, Mondrian and other modern masters.

There is no way back. The alliance of true art and contemporary architecture in an artificial setting is the logical development of the new image-driven and image-consuming global culture, contradicting the argument that original works and reproductions are incompatible. High-profile 'wow!' architects have been working for the Disney group for the past two decades. Even the casino moguls of Las Vegas will opt for top-name architects when they decide to update their phantasmagorias.

The issue can be approached in a different way by looking at the new hotel oases in far-flung, exotic regions of the globe. What is more honest: the graceful Rajvilas – a deceptively 'genuine' simulation in the fairytale world of Rajasthan – or the brave concrete modernism of Four Seasons Sayan in the picturesque mountains of Bali? Which is more beautiful or more culturally appropriate?

The American novelist Mario Puzo describes Las Vegas as 'a place of refuge from reality, from impending worries, from true feelings'. The last part of this statement is arguably wrong, for the feelings are real, irreplaceable. The consumer as traveller seeks distraction and edification, and experiences illusions as actual happenings: the creation of authenticity becomes an art form in itself. This is not a new idea. The German classicist Friedrich Schiller summed it up as early as 1795: 'Indifference to the reality and an interest in the illusion represent a true expansion of humanity and a decisive step towards culture.'

designer & art hotels

The idea may be an old one, but it is still up to producing a few surprises. The head-on encounter with an original interior – one that obeys no other laws than the stylistic dictates of an autonomous designer – continues to exercise a powerful attraction. And the leading figures of the revolution in hotel design – which now dates back more than a decade – are still setting the pace in terms of quality. Yet the focus is no longer on the static innovation of forms and spaces. The creative interest is now focused on giving a dynamic impetus to interior design, adding an emotional dimension to the experience of space – generated by images borrowed from the media, variable lighting effects and illusionistic decorative techniques. The aim is to seduce and captivate guests, in ways that are sublime and subtle, overpowering and imperceptible. In order to achieve these effects, their creators shamelessly plunder the methodological treasure trove of contemporary art – although they only rarely use original art works as part of their designs. Yet perhaps these purist interior landscapes blur the boundaries between image and space, between theatre and life, in a similar way.

land of the pure

The Hotel

Lucerne, Switzerland
2000

Architecture/Interior design: Architectures
Jean Nouvel

above
Jean Nouvel was commissioned by a Lucerne restaurateur to entirely redesign the interior of the six-storey building.

left
Rooms with a view: large, erotically themed movie images are projected onto the ceilings.

IN ancient times, the performance of a great Greek drama was followed by a frivolous play about satyrs. Similarly, in today's classical concerts, a heavy symphonic programme is often rounded off on a lighter note, with a witty capriccio or the like. The commission for The Hotel in Lucerne – which more or less fell into Jean Nouvel's lap after the triumph of his epoch-making Lucerne Arts and Congress Centre – has something in common with this model.

Urs Karli, a prominent figure on the local restaurant scene, who also owns several hotels, engaged the celebrated Paris-based architect to renovate and entirely redesign the interior of a six-storey corner building in the city centre. After the persistent bureaucratic wrangles generated by the big arts complex, one that was really too lavish for a city that is neither large nor especially wealthy, Nouvel must have seen the small hotel project as a welcome, relatively relaxed study, based on themes that had long preoccupied him. One of these themes is removing boundaries by displacing the internal and external perceptions of a building; the experience of space is another. Yet another is the creation of puzzles using space and images. These concepts may sound complicated, but they underlie aspects of all his buildings, and they have never been given such accessible expression as in The Hotel.

This 25-room edifice is aptly named because it demonstrates what the hotel genre is all about. The building, which dates from 1907, appears hollowed out, with empty-looking window sockets. At night, the windows are lit up – and passers-by who look up to the guest floors can witness risqué scenes: blown-up projections of erotic clips from a number of Nouvel's favourite films decorate the ceilings, illuminated by uplighters. The myth of the hotel – the secrets and obsessions of a privacy that has been paid for, combined with cinematic fantasies – could not be given more graphic or more philosophical expression. The voyeur's involvement is permitted only while the guests have nothing to hide. There are no curtains, so guests have to close the folding shutters to end the show.

'Why, for more than a century,' asks Nouvel, 'has architecture abandoned its relationship with the image, with representation, with photography, whereas earlier it used its relationship with painting? I use two-dimensionality to create confusion in space.' In other parts of The Hotel, he shows how this works without the assistance of Buñuel, Bertolucci, Almódovar, Lynch, Fassbinder, Fellini, Greenaway or Oshima. From the bar, guests are given fragmentary, sometimes reflected views into the basement restaurant. Guests watch other guests, but the full truth of the live images remains hidden from them.

The architect took these themes even further in his next hotel project: the River Hotel, located directly under Brooklyn Bridge in New York, where guests stay in rooms with cinemascope windows and one of the world's most famous film sets flickers through the glass: the skyline of Manhattan.

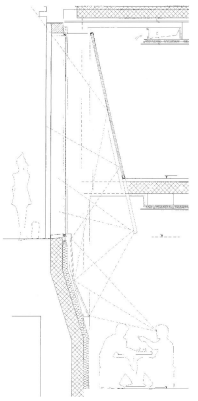

above
The basement restaurant:
large glass sections and
mirrors reflect the dining
scene.

left
Section drawing showing
the covert perspectives
offered to passers-by and
guests.

opposite
Reception (above) and
lobby area (below):
cubic armchairs, bar and
desk are all designed by
architect Jean Nouvel.

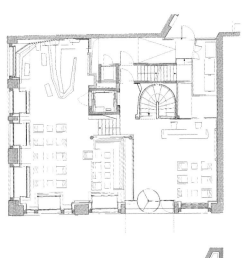

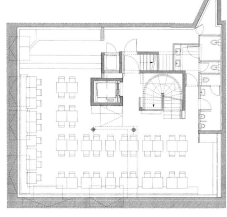

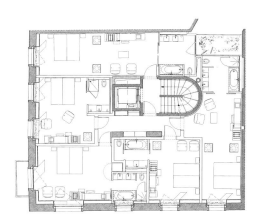

Sanderson

London, UK
2000

Interior design: Philippe Starck

FAMILIAR to anyone who knows about the world of furnishings and interior design, Sanderson is the name of the British company, founded in 1860, which achieved fame for its floral fabrics and carpets, and in particular for its collections based on designs by William Morris. Sanderson's former Soho headquarters, built in 1958, has now been transformed into a hotel by the designer Philippe Starck, his second in London. Both the building and the internal courtyard, created by landscape gardener Philip Hicks, are officially protected from alteration and demolition, which actually encouraged Starck's love of bricolage effects.

According to Starck's long-term client Ian Schrager, who has collaborated with his favourite designer on a succession of projects since the late 1980s, the Sanderson marks a significant new departure: 'We are passionate about continuing to reinvent the idea of the hotel, coming up with breakthrough concepts and going off onto uncharted territory. Sanderson represents the first hotel of the new wave – a hotel for people who crave something original, different and magical. When we thought about doing a true 'urban spa' in London, we wanted to create a completely integrated environment devoted to physical, emotional and spiritual well-being in an exquisitely beautiful setting. The feeling it evokes is one of a genuine sanctuary.... Come to London for the cure.' Whether body and soul can be cured of all civilization's ills at the Sanderson remains open to debate.

Starck's two London hotels are very different in terms not only of thematics but also of composition. St Martin's Lane (see pages 28–33) recalls the spirit of late Romanticism – playing, like Offenbach, with humour, satire and deeper meanings – whereas the Sanderson is more reminiscent of the dream-like weightlessness of Debussy's L'Après-midi d'un faune. Translucent curtains, rather than walls, separate the reception and the restaurant areas on the ground floor. The internal courtyard has become an outdoor lobby. The baths in the 150 guest rooms and suites are set behind glass walls; guests who wish to be hidden while bathing can press a button to close white or pink curtains.

On the floor by the huge silver bed in each guest room

left
Theatrical effects: entrance to the Purple Bar, covered in Venetian mirrors and draped in rich fabrics.

opposite
Urban spa: luxurious remedies for body and soul distinguish the Sanderson from other Starckian hotels. In the Agua Bathhouse waiting area, classical chairs surround a mysterious, glimmering cone.

is a rug with a quotation from Voltaire woven into it; on the ceiling is a magnificent, tastefully framed landscape painting. This time, Starck's eclecticism digs deep into the treasure trove of theatrical props: Venetian mirrors, in the style of a French boudoir from Louis XV to Empire, Dali's bright-red-lips sofa, hand-carved African chairs – a real hotchpotch.

The promised spa experience is supplied by the Agua Bathhouse, which is far bigger and more opulently furnished than its earlier counterpart in Schrager's Delano Hotel in Miami Beach. Starck designed outsized meditation couches with built-in video screens; his steam bath is inflamed with rich colours; the changing areas are decorated with Louis XV armchairs and Venetian engraved mirrors. The magnificent jacuzzi is made of stainless steel.

The hotelier's wife Nornona Schrager is in charge of the holistic health programme designed to satisfy the hotel guests' every whim and desire; its offerings include lymphatic drainage, reflexology, yoga, shiatsu, Thai bodywork, Reiki, meditation. If guests find that all this healthy pampering arouses an equally healthy appetite, they can sample the exquisite gastronomic delights offered by the hotel's Spoon+ restaurant, where the menu was created by none other than the top French chef Alain Ducasse.

above
Eyes wide shut: the backlit Long Bar in the Sanderson, with Cyclops-like stools.

left
Perplexity reigns: in the guest rooms, landscape paintings look down on the beds, with just glass and light curtains surrounding the bath.

opposite
Time travel: the lobby, furnished with objects from different periods and framed by translucent curtains, becomes a dreamscape full of connotations and memories.

Side Hotel

Hamburg, Germany 2001	Architect: Alsop Störmer Interior designer: Matteo Thun

DESPITE its prime position in the centre of Hamburg, Side Hotel, which opened in spring 2001, is surrounded by the shabbiness common to many city centres of the former West Germany that were rebuilt in the postwar period. Although it is just two minutes on foot from the Hamburg opera house, within easy reach of the upmarket shopping and office districts around the Alster, the hotel is directly opposite a dilapidated multi-storey car park, with faceless commercial buildings all around.

Bold architecture was the only solution in such a situation – and the angular hotel building, erected on an irregular plot, marks itself out from its desolate setting with uncompromising clarity. The building has two sections: an eight-storey glass corner structure, and a rear wing, clad in greenish-grey stone, four storeys higher. This hard modernism, combining construction technology and formal incisiveness, is the hallmark of the Hamburg architect Jan Störmer, who collaborated for many years with the British architect William Alsop. Störmer's structure

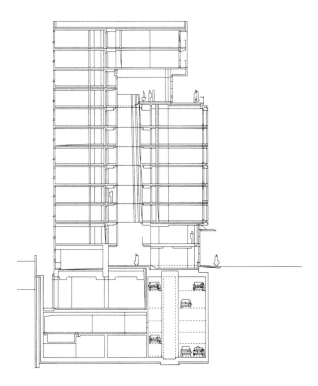

forms a protective shell against the building's environment and creates an effective backdrop for an unconventional hotel concept. A narrow corridor leads into an atrium that is scarcely any wider: a narrow, elongated, empty triangle towering up to an incredibly steep 24 metres (79 feet). Extending upwards over the full height of the structure is a matte glass surface – slightly tilted, to crown it all – illuminated with white light and blue stripes of light which modulate at a strikingly slow rate. The atrium installation was created by US artist Robert Wilson, a magician of contemporary theatre, a master of stage works that combine movement, language, music and light, who has frequently worked in Hamburg.

The drama of this spatial gesture harmonizes perfectly with the general atmosphere of the hotel, whose interiors were stage-managed – in every detail, right down to table decorations and menus – by the designer and architect Matteo Thun of Milan. Thun's motto might have been 'Zen meets Pop', given the mischievous, skilful and cheerfully insolent way he combines period references in a uniquely individual creation. Nothing here is off-the-peg; everything is carefully considered, amazingly comfortable and – with a few colourfully overdone exceptions – a real feast for the eyes. As Thun explains, the effects he achieved were entirely intentional: 'Every ambience is a made-to-measure atmosphere, worlds of sensation with the highest degree of individuality. We wanted to create a hospitality that can be experienced through all the senses. Sensuality through pleasure for the senses.'

The Fusion restaurant and bar on the ground floor (with a separate entrance on the street) and the conference area on the first floor have a cool, classic air. The lower basement, with its swimming pool and health and fitness area, is more colourful. The 178 rooms and suites display a host of innovative touches and a beguiling attention to detail. Thun's particular talent is to make an entirely new way of doing things seem totally natural; one searches in vain for the empty flourishes that are more or less par for the course in other designer hotels.

opposite top
Conceptual drawings of lobby space, with tilted walls (left), and of eighth-floor lounge.

opposite bottom
Soft pebbles: seating area on guest-room level, overlooking the lobby space, with Super Sassi upholstered furniture designed by Matteo Thun.

left
Section of the Side Hotel: the front wing rises to the eighth- floor sky lobby, above which two floors of penthouse suites protrude. Conference facilities, spa and parking are located below street level.

next spread
Basement heaven: the pool area and spa rooms are brightly coloured and sensitively lit to avoid any cavernous feeling the low ceilings might create.

left
Fusion dining: the restaurant, equipped with a sushi bar, occupies a corner of the ground floor.

below left
Drawing of the ground floor: restaurant and hotel have separate street entrances. The narrowing triangular void is the lobby space.

below
Red love: section of the bar, with window onto the hotel entrance.

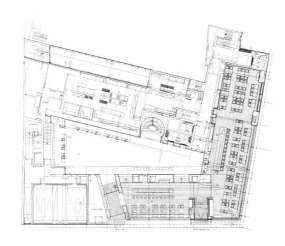

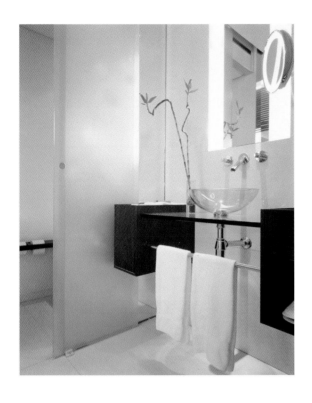

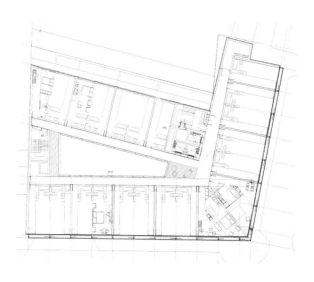

above
Immaterial world: in the standard bathrooms, sliding door, wash basin, and shelf are all made of glass.

above right
Floor plan of second floor.

right
Lurve curve: behind the huge, curved doors are clothes racks and other storage.

St. Martin's Lane

London, UK	Architecture: Harper Mackay
1999	Interior design: Philippe Starck

IT was only a matter of time before the successful US duo of Ian Schrager and Philippe Starck set their sights on the Old World. Nor was it really a surprise when Schrager, the trend-setting impresario of the hotel business, and design superstar Starck chose London for their coup – for the British capital, more than any other European city, has become a focal point for the jet set and a magnet for major and minor celebrities. So the curtain rose for a performance by the masters in two acts: autumn 1999 saw the opening of St Martin's Lane near Trafalgar Square, followed in spring 2000 by the Sanderson Hotel in Soho.

In St Martin's Lane, even more than in the Mondrian (the California project that directly preceded it), artificial light plays a pivotal role. At night the seven-storey building, built in the 1960s as the headquarters of an advertising agency, becomes a brightly shimmering presence, its façades transformed into a bewildering kaleidoscope by lights projected behind the full-height windows of the guest rooms in a huge range of colours; the lighting controls can be individually adjusted and are located, as part of an interactive lightshow, in the bedheads.

Anyone entering the hotel during the day is met by an array of lighting effects, both subtle and not so subtle. At the main entrance the narrow drum of the revolving door is bathed from above in yellow, and light is used to project a carpet pattern onto the stone floor of the lobby. Directly ahead is a glass wall showing a video of a sky with moving clouds. Later in the day, the Light Bar opens behind this wall – a room bathed in purple, green, yellow and red light, and furnished with an incredibly long white table surrounded by closely packed stools. Here and elsewhere, explains Schrager, it is the intention that guests should feel part of an atmospheric stage-set: 'This smart and modern urban resort further refines the ideas of "hotel as theatre" and "lobby socializing".

St Martin's lobby is a soaring theatrical space, akin to a constantly changing stage-set, with eclectic furnishings and distinctive touches everywhere. It is a cosmopolitan village of six discrete but harmoniously interwoven public spaces.'

All the bar and restaurant facilities are grouped around the reception area. To the left of the Light Bar is the Asia de Cuba restaurant, decorated with photos, bookshelves and a colourful array of bric-a-brac, entered through the Rum Bar. More secluded, in the rear section of the ground floor, are the small Sea Bar – where fresh seafood is prepared in the middle of the circular counter – and the Saint M bistro. The Sidewalk Café, which has an outdoor terrace in the summer, opens onto neighbouring Mays Court. The 204 guest rooms are decorated in the traditional Starck white and furnished in familiar spartan style. One brilliant idea was to use the roof of the one-storey porch structure on the side of the building to create tiny patio gardens attached to individual suites.

Not satisfied with transforming the office block into a hotel theatre, Schrager also bought at the same time the neighbouring Lumière cinema, which had been closed for some years. This will be reopened as Tribeca London, an exclusive venue for film screenings and related events.

above
Kaleidoscope: façade detail of the guest floors, with different colour moods.

opposite
Shiny drinks: the Light Bar on the ground floor is transformed at night into a magic chamber of colour and lighting effects.

left
Spinning around: front entrance to St Martin's Lane.

above
**Plain and simple: corridor
on guest room floor.**

opposite
**Gilded teeth and more:
witty bricolage of
furniture and objects in
the hotel lobby.**

above left
**Wait to be seated:
entrance area of the Asia
de Cuba restaurant.**

above right and right
**Conceptual detail
drawings for Asia de Cuba
restaurant.**

opposite
**Interactive illumination: a
light management system
is built into the wall behind
the bedhead, enabling
guests to control the
changing light colours in
the rooms.**

Hotel Greif

Bolzano, Italy
2000

Architecture/Interior design: Boris Podrecca

FOR the Italian town of Bolzano, the Hotel Greif project was more than just the long-overdue renovation of a historic hotel; it was also a vital piece of urban regeneration. The plan conceived by the Vienna-based architect Boris Podrecca was designed to link two very different districts of the town – the medieval centre and the station area, dominated by 1920s architecture – by redeveloping an entire block. Two newly constructed blocks in white and a rich red colour now flank a two-storey shopping arcade covered with strikingly patterned Cippollino marble. The arcade leads to a small square off the historic Waltherplatz, the original home of the Hotel Greif – first documented as the inn Zum schwarzen Greif in 1526.

Not much of the building's original fabric has been retained behind its restored façade. The entrance was moved and the number of rooms was reduced from 130 to 33. All the catering facilities were removed, except for a breakfast room. Then Podrecca invited young artists from Italy, Austria and Germany to transform each room into a one-off work of art. AugenLust ('Pleasure for the Eyes') was the slogan for this initiative, undertaken in collaboration with the local Museum of Modern Art. The past does appear in the form of relics in the contemporary artists' interiors – drawings by 19th-century masters, or Biedermeier and Thonet furniture belonging to the Greif's historic collections.

Podrecca, who has worked on a variety of hotel projects, makes his mark through close attention to detail in terms of both materials and style. In this case he was able to establish a consistent style across the entire project, from architectural fabric to fixtures and fittings. This was made possible by the fact that the investor and the hotel owner were one and the same person, Franz Staffler. Indeed, Staffler's family has owned the historic inn since 1816. Among its famous regulars was the poet Ezra Pound, who lived in nearby Meran from 1958 and immortalized the hotel in his Cantos.

Some of the guest rooms in the restored Greif have whirlpools and saunas – but everyone staying here has to make do with bed and breakfast accommodation. The reason for this is that Staffler also owns another hotel just around the corner, the Parkhotel Laurin, which was smartened up in the early 1990s and is now famed for its restaurant. Parkhotel Laurin was also designed by Podrecca, in collaboration with the architect Albert Mascotti.

Podrecca once said, 'In the transfigured historic setting of a town, the best places will always be those where people are able to dwell amidst uncertainties without feeling a nervous compulsion to look for facts and reasons.' This is the kind of place he has created in Hotel Greif.

above
New urban quarter: Hotel Greif's sundeck overlooks the glazed mall, which stretches between two blocks of Podrecca's multi-purpose complex.

opposite
Minimalist statement: inside the historic hotel contemporary elements, like the staircase leading to the guest rooms, play an important role.

left
Landmark for centuries: the hotel building occupies a corner site on Bolzano's Waltherplatz. The new entrance was moved to the side street.

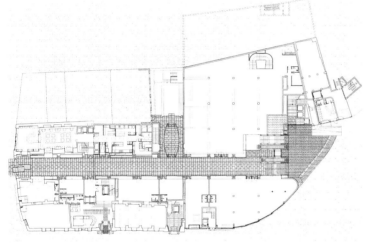

top
Wallpaper artwork by Florin Kompatscher.

above
Ground floor plan.

top right
Art installation by Andrea Fogli.

above right
Art installation by Manfred Alois Mayr.

opposite
Art project: a collaboration with young artists from different countries turns the guest rooms into unique environments. The displays on walls and ceiling are by Arnold Mario dall' O from Italy.

The Standard

| Los Angeles, USA 1999 | Interior design: Shawn Hausmann |

FOR the fashionable American hotel owner André Balasz, The Standard was the second venture in Los Angeles. Following his legendary revamp of the huge Chateau Marmont on Sunset Strip in the early 1990s, Balasz – often compared with his more successful competitor Ian Schrager – opened the off-beat Standard just a few hundred metres away in 1999.

The three-storey hotel building, which opened in 1962 as the Thunderbird motel, had become an old people's home (with its name changed to the more appropriate Golden Crest). Balasz appointed as interior designer Shawn Hausmann, known for his loud set designs for films such as *The People vs. Larry Flynt*. Even though it is not particularly radical, Hausmann's transformation of the building recalls the flower-power world of cinematic spy Austin Powers, combining as it does the original Swinging Sixties backdrop with pop clichés and elements of performance art and club culture. This cheeky remix exerts a magnetic appeal on Balasz's target customers. 'The way people travel, the way people live, the way people communicate – all have changed,' he says. 'People's sophistication far exceeds their wallets these days, and this is an attempt to address the desires of a younger

group of sophisticates. The aim of The Standard is to bring a sense of playfulness and fun and interest to a level of hotel that has not seen any kind of innovation in decades.'

The cheaper of the 140 rooms – furnished with a silver bean-bag, inflatable Ikea sofa and Warhol-flower curtains, and offering high-speed internet access – cost less than US$100. Along with the usual refreshments, the minibars contain such useful items as aphrodisiac drinks and Vaseline. But the real action takes place in the public areas. At night a DJ takes up residence behind the reception desk in the lobby, where an illuminated vitrine is occupied by scantily clad performance artists. During the day another performer vainly struggles to mow the ultramarine artificial lawn on the pool deck. Tattoos and body piercing are on offer in the hotel's own hairdressing salon, an offshoot of the high-class grunge chain Rudy's Barbershop from Seattle. The restaurant and bar are open around the clock.

Investors in the hotel include the film stars Leonardo di Caprio and Cameron Diaz and members of the pop group Smashing Pumpkins. Backed by these and other high-profile names, Balasz plans to open more Standards in Chicago and New York.

right
Out of the blue: the artificial, brightly coloured lawn turns the sundeck into a surreal landscape.

opposite
Live performance: in the glass case behind the reception desk, part-time actors take a nap and stage an irritating welcome to the guests.

Retreat for lounge lizards: the Standard bar recaptures the glory of the old motel, with photo wallpaper and egg-shaped wicker chairs.

left
Must-haves: the rooms are furnished in light wood, the curtains feature prints by Andy Warhol.

opposite
Swinging Sixties: the Standard lobby, with comfortable classics by Ligne Roset, lush flokati carpet and famous Arco lamp designed by Achille Castiglioni.

The Hudson

| New York, USA 2000 | Interior design: Philippe Starck |

IT was in Manhattan in the mid-1980s that the revolution in hotel design began, when Ian Schrager – who had previously achieved local celebrity on account of his trendy nightclubs and his unpaid tax bills – opened the legendary Morgans, designed by Andrée Putman. Soon after this came the Royalton and the Paramount, which laid the foundations of a lasting creative partnership between Schrager and the eclectic design genius Philippe Starck.

After Schrager and Starck had put their energies into high-profile hotel projects in Florida, California and London, they knew that their return to New York – where the world of design had become ever more competitive – would arouse high expectations. They set out to convert a 22-storey brick-built tower erected in 1928 as a clubhouse and hostel for the American Women's Association, and more recently used as the headquarters of the television company Channel 13. The building did not have a name of its own, so Schrager named the new hotel after the river that stands as an emblem of New York City.

The Hudson sets new standards simply in terms of its scale. With 1000 rooms, it is the largest hotel in the Schrager chain, and the conversion costs of more than US$125 million also exceeded the entrepreneur's usual budget. In the Sanderson in London, Schrager and Starck had tried out the luxury version of their 'urban spa' concept; in the Hudson, the delights of a spa retreat can be enjoyed at lesser expense. Admittedly, in most rooms, guests have to put up with the ship's cabin look, in terms of both style and dimensions, but this enhances their appreciation of the magnificently presented public areas.

The visitor's first impression of the Hudson, when double doors slide back to reveal the sober vestibule, is deceptive. Its downbeat plainness is deliberate: the hotel's impact unfolds in a dramatic journey from exterior to interior, as guests are carried upwards on two steep escalators, through a yellowish-green illuminated tunnel, to the large hall at the top of the building. Here, real ivy grows thickly under the tall conservatory roof; the oak reception counter is 20 metres (66 feet) long, and above it hangs an imposing chandelier – designed by the lighting artist Ingo Maurer – which has 56 arms, each one fitted with a hologram bulb.

Starck uses dramatic contrasts of scale and touches of comic exaggeration in the Hudson cafeteria, with its open kitchen and huge wooden tables, and in the library, which is reminiscent of a Batman film set, with its magnificent gas-powered open fireplace, hulking great billiards table, lit by another Maurer creation, and densely packed bookshelves reaching right up to the high ceiling. The Hudson bar also breaks records in terms of size; arranged on a floor of backlit glass tiles is an eclectic collection of furniture, including Louis XV armchairs covered with phosphorescent fabrics and an unfinished tree trunk with boards set into it as a backrest. The imposing ceiling fresco in the bar is the work of the Italian Transavanguardia star Francesco Clemente.

As in the Sanderson, the centrepieces of this Schrager city oasis are its green spaces, including a roof garden that functions as a private park, and a health spa, the two-storey Agua Bathhouse. The Hudson also offers a vast range of sports facilities: basketball and volleyball courts, a bowling alley, a boxing ring, an archery range and an Olympic-size pool. Schrager set out to create on his home territory 'an exciting urban adventure that provides a unique experience'. He believes that 'Style is something you live – it is a basic and profound choice we make every day. Hudson, the ultimate lifestyle hotel, is an outgrowth of this philosophy – where "you are where you sleep" because where you sleep says to the world, "This is who I am."'

The next business idea dreamt up by the pair is Schrager & Starck merchandizing, by which design articles and fashion accessories under the new cult brand will be offered to the hotel's increasing number of fans. They will be distributed not only in lobby boutiques but also by mail order and through a fast-growing chain of dedicated stores.

left
Yellow is the new black:
the hotel entrance is a
rather modest opening
in a grand, bright-yellow
façade.

below
Escalators to the lobby:
through a narrow tunnel
of light, guests are
transported onto the
impressive reception
level. The glass roof
is redolent of a
conservatory and is
covered with real ivy.

above
Conceptual drawing of the
library space illustrates
Philippe Starck's playful
shifting of scale.

left
The Hudson bar:
the dramatically underlit
floor turns the watering
hole into a vibrant stage.
The giant fresco
on the ceiling is a major
work by Italian
Transavanguardia artist
Francesco Clemente.

right
Cabin look:
the rather small standard
rooms are designed in a
restrained maritime
manner, offering nothing
more than the essentials.

THE Milan-based architect Aldo Rossi did not live to see the opening of his second Japanese hotel. In September 1997, six months before the Mojiko was completed, he died from injuries sustained in a car accident. The Japanese interior designer Shigeru Uchida, his partner on the project, remembers the local research they undertook together: 'Architecture can never escape the pervading spirit of a place, regardless of whether it seeks assimilation or confrontation. Aldo Rossi and I walked the town, probing fragments of what had been. These fragments were vessels filled with memories. We examined their images, much like archaeologists, as we formed our hypothesis. To introduce new architecture here, we began to realize, though it would not unlock the fragments, would still plant a new story, and thus create continuity with them.'

The story that the Italian Rationalist and founder of architettura metafisica (the architectural equivalent of Giorgio de Chirico's paintings) wanted to tell at Mojiko was based on the idea of transition. The architectural ensemble – consisting of an eight-storey brick wing and a six-storey stone-clad cube resting on a wide balustrade base – marks the transition between land and sea, creating a pivotal point of reference between the railway station and the ferry dock that connects the island of Moji with the Japanese mainland. The austere monumentality of the façades, perforated with square window openings and combined with the symmetrical proportions typical of Rossi, gives the new building a symbolic quality. The hotel also fulfils the town-planning objectives defined by the specially created public–private financing company: to pave the way for the renovation and regeneration of Moji harbour, both in tourist terms and according to a wider perspective.

Rossi had worked closely with Japanese designer Uchida on his first Japanese hotel, Il Palazzo in Fukuoka (1989) – although for that project Uchida had had to share the interior design role with a group of eminent European colleagues. Here in Mojiko he had a free hand, designing all the interiors himself. Finding the familiar within the strange is one of the essential elements of hotel design as a genre,

left
Overlooking the harbour: Rossi's impressive composition symbolizes the renaissance of Moji Island.

opposite
East meets west: Uchida's interior design of the *Ichiju-An* or tea room relates strongly to a modern interpretation of Japanese aesthetics.

left
Site plan (top) and plan of a typical guest-room floor (bottom).

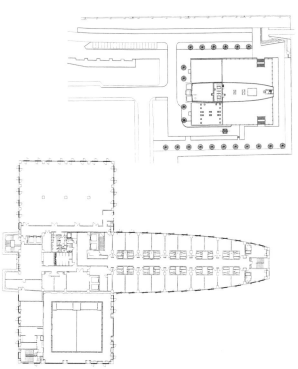

and it could also be described as the leitmotif of Uchida's entire design strategy. The reception and restaurant areas of the Mojiko are neutral and abstract in effect, with one exception: the contemporary/Japanese subtlety of the tea room. Business people are the hotel's target clientele, except at weekends, and the transitory nature of their stays is perfectly reflected in the subdued, reserved character of the interiors.

above
Lobby square: the rigid formalism of the lounge is miles away from the idea of a hotel as a 'home away from home'.

opposite
Over the counter: Bar Tempo, with its dark red interior, offers great views of Moji harbour.

Atoll Hotel

Heligoland, Germany 1999	Architecture: NPS Architekten Nietz, Prasch, Sigl; Alison Brooks Architects Interior design: Alison Brooks Architects

HELIGOLAND has survived a good deal of upheaval. This red, rocky island near the mouth of the River Elbe was once a strategic outpost for the German navy; after 1945 the Royal Air Force made extensive use of the evacuated island as a bomb-testing area. Finally, in the 1950s, civilization was restored and the new Heligoland was built in a plain and functional style, according to an overall masterplan. Today the 1950s buildings are officially protected as a fine example of 'democratic architecture'. The island also experienced its own economic miracle: declared a duty-free zone, it became a popular destination for bargain shoppers and day trippers.

Travellers lured by tax-free alcohol and cigarettes are hardly a prime target for upmarket hoteliers. So how did the Atoll Hotel come to be built in Heligoland? Once again, the responsibility lies with a lone entrepreneur, the Hamburg shipowner and property developer Arne Weber, who himself comes from Heligoland. Weber wanted to set a marker for the future while at the same time making a link with the island's distant past – the 19th-century *fin de siècle*, when a more refined clientele went there for the beneficial effects of the climate and the spa waters.

The external design of the hotel was subject to strict building regulations, so real innovation was only possible inside. In selecting as interior designer the Canadian architect Alison Brooks, who until 1996 had been a partner in designer Ron Arad's studio in London, Weber made the perfect choice. Brooks had played a major role in converting Arad's expressive furniture sculptures into organic-dynamic spatial forms.

The Heligoland hotel project remains true to the stylistic language Brooks had developed in conjunction with Arad, while at the same time showing a high degree of originality in its design solutions. The nearby ocean was taken as a point of reference in every possible way in the interior of the L-shaped hotel, which is located between the harbour and the town hall square. Brooks wanted to achieve an 'architecture that echoed the undersea world of hovering jellyfish, sea flora and watery depths' – and the idea of swimming free of master Arad with a nautical-aquatic theme has an appealing kind of logic. In the floor of the reception area, cylindrical metal pillars have been installed, between which the gently moving water of the basement swimming pool can be seen. The glass outer shell of the bistro annexe is in the form of a drop of water. In the lobby and elsewhere, ceilings are curved in the style of ship's holds, and a circular, translucent skylight looms above the circular bar counters, like an open mussel.

The subtly varied lighting, designed by the architect in collaboration with the Hamburg lighting consultant Peter Andres, enhances the impact of the sculptural spatial features and the wide spectrum of colours. Andres and Brooks also achieved subtle effects in the 50 guest rooms and suites, where the beds are illuminated by backlit head sections. Brooks invented a multi-functional piece of furniture for these rooms: 'Shelf life' – a 7.5 metre (246 foot) long, curving-shelf system incorporating storage space, TV console, minibar, desk, wardrobe and couch; the last of these, with its cowskin cover, pays homage to Le Corbusier. The usual hotel outfitters were unable to provide the engineering expertise needed to produce this amazing creation, so in the end it was supplied by a British firm which produces lightweight components for offshore oil rigs.

opposite
Regular vernacular: the new hotel, following Heligoland's building regulations, is in keeping with the modest 1950s surroundings.

below
Organic shapes: lobby space of the Atoll hotel, with cylindrical centrepiece – a viewing hole into the basement pool.

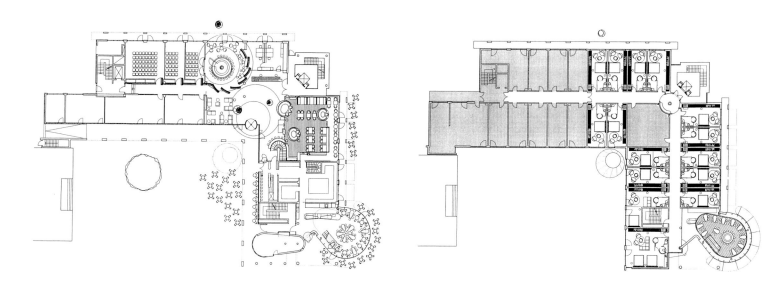

top
Get around: circular table on the upper level of the café and restaurant annexe.

above
Floor plans: ground floor (left) and first floor.

left
Splash area: recreational facilities are situated in the basement.

opposite
Nautical theme: view from lobby to the bar. Above the round bar counter hovers a cylindrical well of light, echoing the form of a shell or a submarine hatch.

above
Spatial geometrics: the rectangular shapes of the bed area contrast with the curved ceiling above the sculptural, built-in bathroom area.

right
At your convenience: one of the hotel's rest rooms.

opposite (top and bottom)
Innovative rack: the multi-functional wall-element serves as storage, TV shelf and lounge rest with a touch of Le Corbusier. The drawing below gives a full explanation of unit.

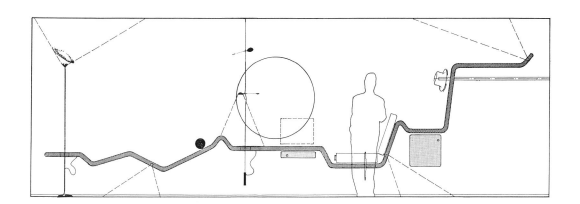

The Mercer

New York, USA 1998	Interior design: Christian Liaigre

THE long and difficult gestation of New York's Mercer Hotel could be described as a progression from black comedy to bravura display. The hotel was grandly announced, as a luxury residence incorporating cutting-edge design, in the early 1990s, but then the hotel owner André Balasz had to grapple with a major property recession and countless other obstacles – including the assassination of his project manager. The work on the hotel even came to a halt for a long period before everything suddenly took a miraculous turn for the better. The sources of finance began to flow freely; the design contract was reassigned to French interior and furniture designer Christian Liaigre; and even before the official opening film stars and and other celebrities were queueing up to stay in the Mercer. Balasz's wife Katie Ford, the director of a leading model agency, knew how to give the high-profile clientele what they wanted from a hotel.

André Balasz could hardly have made a better choice than Liaigre to achieve the perfect look for his 75-room, five-star hotel. Liaigre had first come to Balasz's attention in 1991 as the designer of the small, elegant Montalembert Hotel in Paris. His inimitable style, seamlessly combining ethnic influences from Africa or Polynesia with the functional and elegant 'salon' modernism of 1920s Paris, was the ideal recipe for the Mercer's exclusive, understated appeal.

While the project had suffered delays, a great deal had changed in the SoHo area of Manhattan, where the Mercer was located. Within a few years, the neighbourhood had risen to become a vibrant, fashionable centre for the arts, while the Guggenheim Museum's avant-garde offshoot had opened directly opposite the hotel site. In terms of design, Balasz aimed to present in the Mercer a clear alternative to the trend-setting creations of his great model and

competitor Ian Schrager, who had created such contemporary New York design icons as the Royalton and the Paramount, working in collaboration with global design superstar Philippe Starck. 'I wanted to create a hotel with an atmosphere of domestic bliss,' says Balasz. 'It's the opposite of dictatorial. It's very important that when you go to a place you don't have to check your personality at the door. I mean, the purpose of design is to make you feel comfortable. Why should you feel onstage when you sit on a chair?'

Liaigre's interiors undoubtedly feel like comfortable places of refuge. Behind the brilliantly restored brick façade of the neo-Romanesque building – erected as an office block by magnate John Jacob Astor in 1890 – guests are welcomed in an elongated, discreet lobby with a bar and a reading corner. A restaurant called The Kitchen is located in the basement; its name is entirely appropriate in that a third of the tables are located right in the kitchen area (these 'backstage' tables are the most popular of all). The generously proportioned guest rooms, with full-length bow windows, parquet flooring and luxuriously large bathrooms, avoid all frilly ornamentation, radiating a casual and elegant homeliness. 'We wanted to capture the modern loft spirit,' says interior designer Liaigre. 'It's like an elegant studio. It's simple, quiet, chic, what one wants to find in one's own home.'

above
The guest rooms are
generously proportioned,
with full-length windows
and parquet flooring.

above
**One of the main aims
of the hotel is to create a
feeling of homeliness.
'The purpose of design is
to make you feel
comfortable,' says owner
Balasz.**

above left
**The luxuriously large
bathrooms avoid frilly
ornamentation.**

opposite
**'I wanted to create a
hotel with an atmosphere
of domestic bliss,' says
André Balasz, owner of the
Mercer.**

The Ritz-Carlton

| Wolfsburg, Germany, 2000 | Architecture: Henn Architekten
Interior design: Andrée Putman |

WHY Wolfsburg of all places? That must have been the question uppermost in the mind of Horst Schulze, the president of the luxury Ritz-Carlton hotel chain, when the proposal landed on his desk in Atlanta. Wolfsburg, in the north German lowlands, is neither a city nor a holiday destination. Its only claim to fame is as the headquarters of the German car maker Volkswagen and the site of its main factory. The Volkswagen CEO Ferdinand Piech had already overseen the raising of the group's profile through the acquisition of luxury brands such as Bentley and Lamborghini. Now he wanted to secure Volkswagen's place in the international premier league by means of the new hotel, planned as an adjunct to the group's 25 hectare (62 acre) AutoStadt theme park. So Ritz-Carlton was presented with the 'ready-made', five-star proposal on a plate: the whole interior of the hotel designed by Andrée Putman, the *grande dame* of contemporary hotel design, whose work at Morgans in New York had led a renaissance of the genre.

In the summer of 2000, Wolfsburg gained the classiest hotel owned by any car manufacturer, while Ritz-Carlton acquired an outpost in the provinces, a partner for the Ritz-Carlton in Berlin, its first hotel in Germany. The building itself – an open, concave, five-storey ring structure situated north-west of the AutoStadt theme park – was designed by Henn Architekten in Munich, who had

long been responsible for all large-scale projects undertaken by Volkswagen. Despite its distinctive form, the building has all the charm of an upmarket office block – not exactly the most propitious setting for a masterpiece of contemporary hotel design. Yet this is exactly what Andrée Putman has managed to achieve there.

In the Ritz-Carlton at Wolfsburg, Putman has realized her design concepts with more ease, elegance and perfection than in any of her many other hotel interiors. The marvels begin not at reception – a plain, draughty transit zone – but beyond, in the lobby, which is characterized by luxurious upholstery, a large fireplace and a panoramic view over the harbour basin and the old brick power station. It is immediately obvious what the designer was trying to do. 'The architecture of the building, the playing with a curve, was what made me soften my style, which had always been a little extreme. I was particularly interested in creating a place of grace and quiet on an industrial site,' says Andrée Putman. The choice of colours and materials in the lounge, and above all the subtle diversity of the lighting – floor-to-ceiling wall sections encased in metal fabric or covered with thin stone slabs are used as light fittings – create a stunning impact. Opening off the lounge to left and right are a shop, a bar, restaurants and conference rooms. Each area has its own individual style, carefully reproduced in even the smallest details, while at the same time remaining closely integrated with the restrained character of the whole.

On the guest floors Putman again worked within the architectural constraints of the building. The corridors are curved cabin-style passageways, while the 174 rooms and suites are oases of privacy and seclusion. Ritz-Carlton, which is more commonly associated with traditional old-fashioned luxury, demonstrates in its hotel at Wolfsburg that contemporary design is capable of producing the highest standards of comfort and décor – as long as the designer is a top talent such as Andrée Putman, and a confident owner such as Volkswagen is prepared to give her a free hand.

opposite
Lush masterpiece: the restaurant has its own individual style, while remaining integrated with the design of the whole.

left
Curved building: the Ritz-Carlton hotel is part of the ambitious automotive theme park that Volkswagen has placed next to its main car plant.

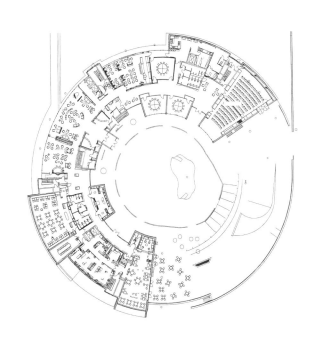

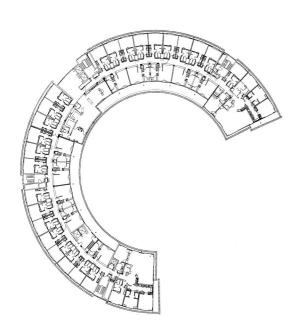

opposite
Lounge bar: part of the spacious lobby area is this intimate meeting point for pre- or post-business talks.

above left
Oasis of privacy: Putman proves that contemporary design is capable of producing the highest standards of comfort and décor.

above
Suite dreams: living room and adjoining study in one of the presidential suites.

left
Floor plans of ground floor (left) and typical guest-room floor.

business hotels

THE new generation of business hotels, large and small, exhibits two clear design trends. On one hand, the high-profile hotel chains are discovering that distinctive contemporary interior design gives them an edge in the five-star marketplace. In the past, opulence and monotonous neutrality were the keynotes of the largely faceless executive hotels; today, by contrast, a thoroughly audacious modernity is becoming more widespread. The mainstream is turning stylish and its polyglot clientèle values the increasing individuality of city-centre residences trading under familiar group names. On the other hand, in many places, individual hotel developers are boldly investing in abandoned, neglected and forgotten properties – and achieving magnificent results through stylistic finesse rather than lavish budgets.

city chic

IF the hotel's name sounds familiar, its distinctive design would leave the expert onlooker in no doubt that this classy small hotel on Amsterdam's Keizersgracht was the work of Lady Weinberg, better known as London-based fashion and interior designer Anouska Hempel. 20 years ago, she opened the ornate Blakes Hotel in London and in 1996 created its Zen counterpart, The Hempel, also in London. Her third excursion into the hotel business began when a fan of the original Blakes came into the possession of an historic site in Amsterdam but could not decide what to do with it.

Relatively large for the old city of Amsterdam, the site incorporates five 18th-century buildings set around an internal courtyard dating from 1637, when a theatre was founded there. Plays by Shakespeare, Molière, Voltaire and Corneille were among those staged at the theatre over the years; at its centenary celebrations in 1737 the orchestra was conducted by none other than Antonio Vivaldi, and foreign celebrities in the audience included the Czar of Russia. In 1772 the theatre was destroyed by fire. Only the sandstone portico – now the main entrance of the hotel – survived the flames. The old brickwork seen today dates from a later period, when the building belonged to the Catholic Old Poor People's Office founded by wealthy families in the city. The gourmet restaurant Blakes now occupies the institution's former bakery, dating from 1787; the lounge was once the food store.

Anouska Hempel took great care to design and furnish the other spaces and facilities – 26 rooms and suites, bar, conference rooms and private dining rooms – in a style that is sympathetic to the building's historic fabric. 'It was always going to be a daunting task to weave a new hotel into an existing environment, without affecting the history, architecture and integrity of the interior spaces,' she says. 'The primary aim was to work with the existing spatial form and detail, taking cues and inspiration from the heavy timber beams, gable, dormer and intricate timber detail, exposed herringbone brick walls and flooring and finely framed fenestration.' To achieve harmony between the old building and her own style, which is dominated by Asian influences, Anouska Hempel chose the golden age of the Netherlands – the era when the nation drew its wealth from its East Indian colonies – as a point of reference for the entire interior design concept. Colours, fabrics and furniture are used in such a way as to link past and present. Hempel also achieves a synthesis in terms of her own work: on Keizersgracht the opulence of the London Blakes and the cool minimalism of The Hempel come together in a masterpiece of restrained luxury.

above
Retreat in the city: inner courtyard of the Amsterdam Blakes Hotel

left
More than bread and butter: the gourmet restaurant is located in the former Catholic welfare institution's old bakery.

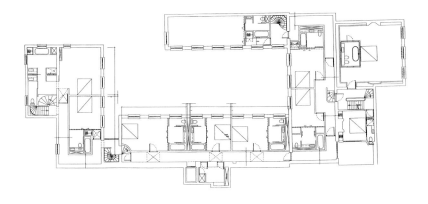

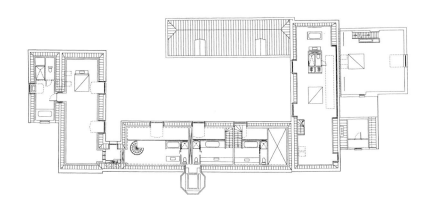

above
Floor plans of two guest-room floors (first and third), which show the new layouts fitted neatly in the untouched historic fabric.

right
A little respect: designer Anouska Hempel took great care to furnish the hotel in a style that was sympathetic to the building's historic fabric.

opposite and above
Nothing the same: each room is decorated and furnished individually, all themed in fabric, style and colour as a reinterpretation of Asian and colonial Dutch influences.

Kirketon Hotel

Sydney, Australia 1999 | Interior design: Burley Katon Halliday Architects

THERE could scarcely be a better location for this smart minimalist city hotel than Darlinghurst. The Kirketon is just a few minutes' walk away from Sydney's main shopping district, the lively King's Cross area and the harbour and opera house. The three-storey 1920s building had been used as a hotel before, but it was then a modest establishment consisting of 60 tiny bedrooms packed closely together with no private bathrooms and minimal facilities.

The investors Terry and Robert Schwamberg – who had already opened a small, chic hotel called the Medusa – decided that much more could be made of the plot of nearly 1800 square metres in this prime location. The local pair entrusted the project to the trendy design team of Burley Katon Halliday. 'The client wanted boutique-style accommodation and facilities; the design imbues it with a subdued urbanism,' says Iain Halliday. 'A whimsical mix of classic 20th century, contemporary and antique furnishings occurs throughout. The real challenge was to

create a sense of seamless division between the many differing functional spaces within one project.'

The architects cleared out the ground floor of the building – not a particularly convenient space in terms of shape, with a fairly deep floor plan and a narrow front to the street – to make room for the lobby and reception (with its adjoining day bar) as well as the Salt restaurant, with its entrance on Darlinghurst Road. The far end of the ground floor, where there was once a row of tiny sleeping dens, now houses a good-sized conference room and the stylish, intimate Fix bar. To make the space seem bigger, a large number of extensive (often wall-to-wall) mirrors have been installed in the lobby, restaurant, corridors and rooms, incidentally creating some surprising perspectives. On the two upper storeys of the building, every third guest room has been sacrificed to create two private bathrooms, one for each of the two neighbouring units. Even now these Junior Rooms are not particularly spacious, so anyone wanting more luxurious accommodation would do better to book one of the Premium or Executive Rooms, at the back of the hotel or on the street side. The hotel houses 40 rooms in all.

In 1999, when the new Kirketon opened, its Salt restaurant and Fix bar were already at the top of the rankings in Sydney – giving the hotel enough advance publicity to establish it as the city hideaway of choice for high-profile Olympics tourists in the late summer of 2000. Since then, it has become a favourite stopover for the cosmopolitan in-crowd who make ever more frequent journeys 'down under'.

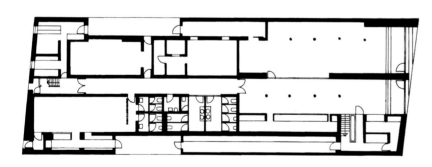

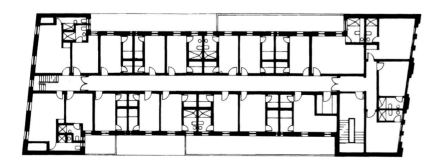

opposite
Narrow lot: floor plans of
the ground floor and
typical guest floor show
the difficult shape of the
site, with a small front and
an elongated back
section.

next spread
Staircase to guest room
floors (left). View into the
Fix bar, a discreet spot
located towards the rear
of the building on the
ground floor (right).

below
Showpiece: lobby and
reception area, with
luxurious couch and big
Cappellini floor lamp.

above
**Straight affair: the design
of the guest rooms opts
for minimalist coolness.**

left
**Mirror, mirror, on the wall:
in the long corridors of the
guest floors, a feeling of
space is created by
simple and efficient
means.**

Fitzwilliam Hotel

Dublin, Ireland 1998	Architecture: Ashlin Coleman Heelan & Partners Interior design: Conran & Partners

ST STEPHEN'S Green, the perfect place to enjoy a leisurely stroll in the heart of Dublin, was given to the city by a member of the Guinness brewing dynasty in 1880. At that time, immaculate Georgian houses lined the park. Less than a hundred years later, many of these historic buildings had fallen victim to property speculation. Nowadays, thanks to the efforts of local heritage groups, more care is taken to preserve the city's traditional architecture, and new buildings have to blend in properly with their historic setting. Dublin's enlightened development strategy has helped re-establish its old centre as a tourist attraction.

An example of a new building that fits in well with its historic surroundings is the Fitzwilliam, a five-star hotel which boldly claims to set new standards in the Irish hotel business. The inconspicuous nine-storey white block is located on the narrow side of St Stephen's Green, not far from where the park meets the upmarket shops of Grafton Street. The personality of this apparently neutral structure becomes apparent only when you look through the large glazed front into the entrance hall. Here the interior designers, Conran & Partners of London, have created a 'baronial modernist' setting in which to welcome guests – a strikingly successful blend of Bauhaus and country house.

'The Fitzwilliam bridges the gap between the traditional and the contemporary,' explain the designers. 'It is both a cosmopolitan landmark in the city and a retreat from its everyday hustle and bustle. It is one of a new breed of hotels that goes against the grain of the multinational hotels of the past two decades. It has a unique and individual character.' In the lobby, inviting armchairs are arranged in front of a large fireplace. Above this, on the mezzanine, is the gourmet restaurant Peacock Alley. The hotel bar, The Inn on the Green, is dominated by an impressive curved counter, representing a modern interpretation of the classic Irish pub. Right at the top of the hotel is a large, well-designed roof garden, created in defiance of the unreliable weather – a testimony to Emerald Isle optimism.

The Fitzwilliam has a total of 137 guest rooms and suites. Their interiors, characterized by neatly worked solid materials and rectangular forms, are inspired by the functional, businesslike luxury of the 1920s. Guests with a view over the park can sit on built-in window seats and watch all the city life from a distance.

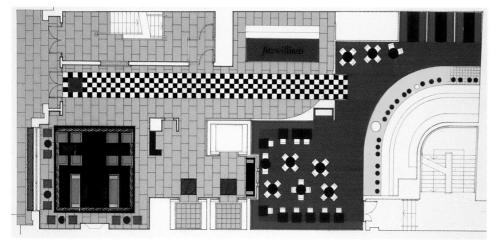

above
Unobtrusive newcomer: the restrained building is located right on Dublin's famous St. Stephen's Green.

left
Floor plan of hotel's street-level public areas.

opposite
Domestic dimensions: lobby with fireplace and cosy upholstery.

above
Sound and solid: the Inn on the Green bar combines traditional Irish values with a touch of contemporary class.

right
Classical note: guest-room interiors try to catch the spirit of the 1920s, while guaranteeing all the comfort of today.

opposite
Well-tempered modernity: entrance hall and reception area.

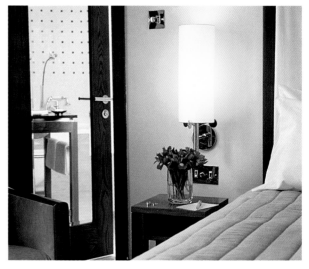

Gastwerk Hotel

Hamburg, Germany	Architecture: Lange und Partner
2000	Interior design: Regine Schwethelm, Sibylle von Heyden

SINCE their closure several decades ago, the gasworks in the Bahrenfelde district of Hamburg, built in 1857, had gradually deteriorated, despite being recast in a variety of undignified guises; most recently, its brick-built halls were used for the manufacture of pet food. But lately some abandoned industrial sites have proved very attractive to investors, especially when they offer low-cost construction land in up-and-coming areas – and the former gasworks is one of these. The Gastwerk Hotel, which opened in early 2000, is a vital element of the regeneration plan for the area – a project dubbed Forum Altes Gastwerk.

The former coal depot – a two-storey saddle-roof hall with no pillars and a four-storey central space – was identified as a suitable setting for the four-star hotel. For the owner and operator Kai Hollmann it was love at first sight: 'It started off as just a mad idea. About five years ago, when we saw the ruins of the old gasworks for the first time, we thought instantly that it should be made into a hotel – a hotel with plenty of space, a distinctive design... something out of the ordinary. But suddenly the idea took on a life of its own. It didn't matter who we told about it, everyone was enthusiastic: architects, conservation authorities, city council – even the tourism associations and our colleagues.'

The conversion costs were nearly 13 million Euros for a total area of 11,350 square metres (122,130 square feet). The high central building became the hotel entrance. Restaurant and conference facilities were located at ground level in the two side wings. Above this are the 100 guest rooms and suites. As far as possible, the industrial character of the building has been preserved; it is evident not only in the bare brickwork of many sections of the walls and parts of the ceiling but also in the remnants of machinery left in their original state.

The style of interior design alternates between openness and intimacy. From the large reception hall with its red carpet and gilt reception desk, guests descend a few stairs to the left into a homely lobby lounge flanked by the bar and the Da Caio restaurant. Opposite, in the right-hand wing, a freestanding, impressively monumental conference table symbolizes the purpose of the meeting rooms on this side of the hotel. Coffee breaks are held in the shade of the old gas processing machine, whose metal framework has survived the ravages of time. The guest-room interiors are dominated by four colour schemes, each designed to elicit a particular emotional response: red and beige for a warm, calming effect; white and natural tones to appeal to contemporary purists; grey, beige and brown for sporty types; dark brown and natural tones for a cosy feel. Most of the furniture was designed by the two Hamburg-based interior designers Regine Schwethelm and Sibylle von Heyden. There is one delightful finishing touch: in place of the usual radio alarm with its complicated programming systems, a basic alarm clock, simple and reliable, stands alone on the bedside table.

above and left
Out of the ruins: it took devotion to turn the disused industrial site (above) into an inviting hotel experience (left).

left
Relics of the industrial age: the iron skeleton of the old gas processing machine (pictured here before restoration) forms a machine-aesthetic backdrop to conference area.

Opposite
Get the point: a long conference table is the key feature of the ground floor's concrete wing.

left
Atrium lobby: the
reception is located in
the central space of
the former gasworks,
which is open right
up to the roof.

above
Early sketch of one of the hotel's suites.

right
Bare bricks: in the guest rooms, as in other parts of the hotel, the original brickwork is preserved and left unplastered, to suggest the industrial origin of the building.

Four Seasons Hotel, Canary Wharf

London, UK	Architecture: RHWL Partnership
1999	Interior design: United Designers

ITS second London hotel marked a daring leap into the world of modern design for the American luxury hotel chain Four Seasons. Before the opening of Four Seasons Canary Wharf in late 1999, the company had been known for its solid classicism. It had already made a departure into Art Deco, but had never ventured into the contemporary realm. The interior was the responsibility of United Designers, who had already completed a number of small hotel and restaurant projects, and in Canary Wharf – where they had a budget of £26 million to design 14,500 square metres (156,000 square feet) – they were in their element.

Canary Wharf is the dynamic heart of London's booming new financial district. In the early 1990s, this redeveloped area of London's docklands was branded the biggest property flop of all time. Less than a decade later, it has become the city's most dynamic business quarter,

with rising rents and new buildings constantly creeping up into the sky. One of these new buildings is Canary Riverside, an 11-storey block with protruding window openings designed by the architects RHWL Partnership. This is the building that houses the Four Seasons, and the designers took the façade's square motif as their point of departure for the hotel's interior: table tops, vases, wall reliefs and light fittings are all square.

The restaurant is called Quadrato. In the foyer, the square, in the form of the cube, becomes the defining element: reception desk, lobby seating area, bar and cloakroom are all based on the same geometry. Keith Hobbs, Principal of United Designers, explains the reasons behind this design solution: 'The cubes appear as four pieces of furniture that have simply been dropped in place. The fact that they do not touch the ceiling creates a feeling of one open space. The aim was to add an element of fluidity and fun to the interior and, with the careful use of lighting, to create areas of intimacy, privacy and seclusion in which guests would want to explore.'

The triple-height entrance hall leads to a bar, a restaurant and the conference areas. The 142 rooms and suites are spread over a total of eight storeys, with the 728 square metre (7,830 square foot) Presidential Suite on the top floor. Light stone and dark wood predominate, while the furniture is deliberately functional. The new Four Seasons has been designed to reflect the distinctly masculine world of finance. Anything cosier would have been incongruous amid the banks and investment houses of Canary Wharf.

above
Canary riverside: the hotel is part of a new development in London's most dynamic business district.

left
Theatre box: seats in the protruding windows of the guest rooms offer magnificent views of the River Thames and the City.

opposite
Glitzy welcome: entrance hall and grand staircase of the Four Seasons Canary Wharf.

above
Lounge cube: just a few steps from the reception desk, a cubic structure forms a room in a room.

left
Floor plans of ground floor (top) and typical guest-room floor (bottom).

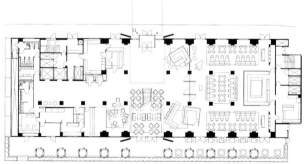

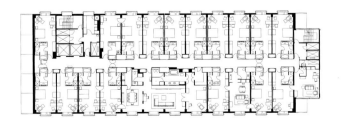

right
**Sober details: the
standard bathroom relies
on an uncompromising
contemporary approach.**

below
**Presidential Suite:
view of lounge and
sleeping areas.**

JÖRG C. Bube, who trained as a banker, seems to have a thing about old, listed religious buildings. The Hopper Hotel St Antonius, opened in 1999, was his second hotel converted from a former Christian institution. The previous project, the Hotel Hopper et cetera, was set in an abandoned monastery building; this one was in a Catholic journeymen's hostel, erected by the Kolping Brotherhood in 1904–05, which had closed in 1997.

As intended by the architects HKR, who were entrusted with the redevelopment, everything about the new four-star residence recalls its former incarnation. 'We developed the idea of refurbishing the existing features and linking these in design terms with the requirements of a modern hotel,' says Rolf Kursawe. 'In many details the design concept returns again and again to the building's original use as a journeymen's hostel.'

The brick and sandstone façade, battered by bombs in the Second World War, was restored in all its detail, as was the roof. Inside, the robust terrazzo and stone floors were preserved as far as possible. The main gate leads straight into the former dining room, now occupied by a branch of the fashionable local restaurant chain Spitz. Only the entrance belongs to the hotel itself, and the foyer and lobby are correspondingly narrow. However, the designers managed to incorporate an elongated, triangular, floor-level pond with goldfish and floating flowers as well as a media box with television, telecommunications facilities and internet access.

Behind the reception counter hangs a magnificent portrait of L. Fritz Gruber of Cologne, a photographic collector and founder of the Photokina world

imaging fair. It was Gruber who added the artistic element to the Hopper St Antonius: works by famous photographers are placed throughout the hotel, including in its 54 rooms and suites, whose ascetic interiors combine functionality with skilful minimalist design. Cuboid shapes predominate in the furnishings, and there is little in the way of colour; white fabrics and paintwork contrast with the natural reddish brown of the woods. The washbasins in the bathrooms, tiled with light grey marble, are reminiscent of sink units in a laboratory. All the suites have kitchenettes. So it is not only the hotel's location – in the shadow of the cathedral tower, to the rear of the main railway station, at the traditional heart of the city – that marks it out for success. In design terms, too, this former journeymen's home from home is perfect for today's visitors, many of whom, in this media-obsessed city, are involved in the television and music business.

Jörg C. Bube has registered the Hopper name as a trademark – one that he hopes will cross language barriers to evoke an image of the style-conscious urban nomad. (It can only be an advantage if it also brings to mind such famous figures as Edward Hopper and Dennis Hopper.) The Hopper boss is currently looking for a property for his next Cologne project. Given that St Anthony is the patron saint of searchers – his statue stands in the inner courtyard of Hopper no. 2 – the third in the series is bound to turn up soon.

right
From brothers to guests: the Hopper St Antonius building is a former Catholic journeymen's hostel.

left
Get the picture: the entire hotel is decorated with works of great photographers. Behind the reception desk, one is greeted by an image of the Cologne-based Nestor of international photo art, L. Fritz Gruber.

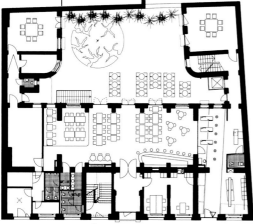

above

**Brain zone with a promise:
conference room looking
onto the courtyard, where
the beer garden is busy in
the summer.**

left

**Plans of the ground floor
and typical guest-room
floor.**

top left
Just sofas: small lobby and indoor entrance to the Spitz restaurant.

top right
Bistro delights: counter and seating area in the Spitz restaurant.

above left
Home for a while: the suites, with living rooms and kitchenettes, cater for long-term guests from the media industry.

above right
Lobbying fish: the narrow pond stretches right through the reception area.

One Aldwych

London, UK 1998	Architecture: Jestico Whiles Associates Interior design: Jestico Whiles Interiors; Mary Fox Linton

IN 1998 a five-star hotel opened on the corner of Aldwych and Strand, a prime London location where the City meets the West End. Although designed to satisfy its guests' every need, the new hotel is restrained and unostentatious in character. When he took on the project at One Aldwych, the entrepreneur Gordon Campbell Gray was inspired by a belief in the virtues of 'stealth wealth', which he had already successfully demonstrated in a number of smaller-scale luxury hotels in the UK and the USA.

The existing building on the site had been erected in 1907 to house the Morning Post daily newspaper, long since defunct. Project architects Jestico Whiles Associates took great care in restoring it to its former grandeur. From the outside, the building remains a classic example of imposing Edwardian architecture, lavishly ornamented

with details in the style of Louis XVI. On the inside, however, decades of office use had resulted in the near-destruction of the original floor plans and ceiling heights.

It is hard to imagine a more exemplary conversion than One Aldwych, for the building's new function and its original character are a perfect match. The project owes its success to a passionate attention to detail combined with technical sophistication. For example, the lobby was opened up to its original height, but without the first vacuum-based waste-water system in London, its dramatic impact would have been considerably diminished by the need to house the pipework serving the guest rooms.

Clever architectural alterations have been made to offset some of the more austere aspects of the original building, such as the rather plain main staircase; in this case, the lifts were moved and the additional space created was used to accommodate a new, wider stairway. The stone façade conceals a steel structure with concrete floors that was very modern at the time it was built; this structure is clearly visible in the basement, where its riveted pillars are an appropriate feature of the keep-fit area, which includes a pool.

In keeping with the client's preference for discretion, all the interiors were designed to be unobtrusive – impressive for their relaxed style rather than for opulence or extravagance. Campbell Gray is especially sensitive to being called 'trendy': 'We don't go down any gimmicky routes at all. I am at pains to avoid the tag of "designer" hotel. I see One Aldwych as a modern classic. It was never meant to be a hotel for young groovy people.'

It may have been impossible to prevent 'young groovy people' taking over the splendid lobby bar, but most of the 105 rooms and suites are now booked by members of the international business jet set. The Dome Suite on the top storey, in particular, is perfect for top executives and business magnates: it includes the room right under the building's dome, which has a table that seats ten, making it the perfect place to conduct discreet negotiations or put the finishing touches to a takeover deal.

left
Splendid conversion: the former press building now houses one of London's poshest hotels.

opposite
Place to be: the lobby of One Aldwych has become a social hotspot for West End aficionados.

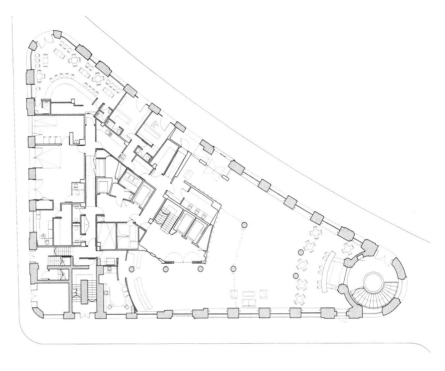

far left
Heavy metal: the stripped old steel pillars make a perfect setting for the new basement pool and gym area.

above
Ground-floor plan of the triangular site, with the generous lobby occupying most of the space.

left
Perfect fit: detail of bathroom in a standard guest room.

Grand Hyatt

| Berlin, Germany | Architecture: José Rafael Moneo |
| 1998 | Interior design: Hannes Wettstein |

ANYONE who wishes to see for themselves the kind of aberration that can result from the attempt to create a 'designer hotel' should head for the Grand Hyatt in Berlin. This luxury hotel – the first of its type in Germany to be built by the US-based Hyatt Group – is located on Potsdamer Platz, where the automotive group Daimler-Chrysler tried its hand at property development, successfully transforming a desolate wasteland (the result of more than four decades of political division) into a vibrant new city district.

As is so often the case with chain hotels, the Grand Hyatt was based on a largely predefined concept. Daimler-Chrysler had commissioned the Spanish architect José Rafael Moneo to design the building, while the interior was entrusted to the Swiss designer Hannes Wettstein. For both Moneo and Wettstein, this was their first hotel project; if proof were needed that even the big names are not immune from the consequences of inexperience, their Potsdamer Platz creation would supply it.

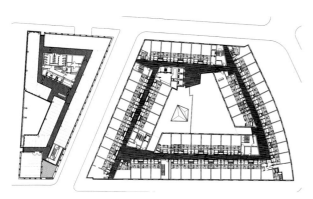

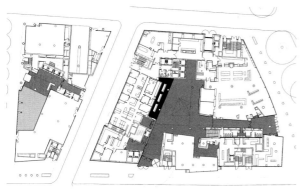

The external shell of red sandstone set with closely packed rows of small windows has all the appeal of a mundane office block. The entrance, the lobby and the gallery on the conference and function floor display a rigid, lifeless minimalism that indicates a sheer lack of ideas rather than architectural rigour. The problem is one of scale. In small buildings, minimalism is a tried and trusted way of demonstrating larger capabilities. However, in a hotel where visitors are dwarfed by barren immensities, the effect is merely oppressive. As they sit in the dark leather seats with light streaming down on them from above, guests at the Grand Hyatt are confronted by a huge empty picture frame hanging high up on the wall, while in the ballroom opalescent bowls of light resemble ordinary lampshades expanded to ten times their normal size.

In his design of the Grand Hyatt, Hannes Wettstein was concerned to reinterpret luxury; his work was based on the concept of 'contemporary elegance and ease that grounds the quality of experience in the location'. A deliberate simplicity characterizes the choice of materials and the formal vocabulary – from the three restaurants and the 340 rooms and suites right through to the health suite on the top storey. The pool area, dubbed Club Olympus, with its south-facing sun deck, offers magnificent panoramas of Berlin.

From the time when John Portman made his first atrium constructions in the late 1960s, pioneering hotel architecture has been a trademark of the Hyatt group – still majority-owned by the Pritzker family, who founded the international architecture prize of the same name. José Rafael Moneo won the Pritzker Prize in 1996, but the hotel group cannot be very happy with the designs produced by Moneo and Wettstein in Berlin. Just 18 months after the opening it was decided gradually to give the interiors a more welcoming face lift. The lobby was the first to be refurbished, in mid-2000, with further renovations planned.

above
Expect the ordinary: Rafael Moneo's Berlin hotel is an architectural understatement in itself.

left
Plans of the ground floor (bottom) and a typical guest-room floor (top).

opposite
Reduced to the max: lounge area with big, empty wall frame, deconstructivist skylight and leather upholstery.

above
How to dwarf the audience: in the ballroom, oversized lampshades hang threateningly from the ceiling.

left
Bauhaus revisited: long bistro table in the Berlin Hyatt by Swiss designer Hannes Wettstein.

WITH more than 80 hotels and holiday resorts in Germany, the Netherlands, Belgium, Switzerland, Austria, Hungary, the Czech Republic and Turkey, the Dorint Group is one of Germany's major players on the international tourism scene. Its fast growth in recent years has led the group to focus on two separate areas of the market, the middle and upper segments, while seeking to present a younger image to the market. The Dorint Budget Hotels concept was devised to attract price-conscious customers, while innovative design was identified as a key factor in upgrading the company's five-star operations.

The prototype for the group's stylish new upmarket range is the Hotel am Gendarmenmarkt in Berlin – a relatively small property with 92 rooms and suites which opened in 1999 – whose instant success inspired another, similar venture. By late 2000 the 216-room designer hotel Dorint am Alten Wall had opened in Hamburg. Converted from a former post office savings bank, the Hamburg hotel building had considerably more superficial appeal than its counterpart in Berlin.

The Berlin hotel has been converted from a prefabricated structure in the Art Nouveau style. Even though it was built as recently as the early 1980s in what was then the capital of the former German Democratic Republic, it is a listed building. It occupies a prominent corner plot directly opposite the unique Prussian classicist ensemble of Karl Schinkel's Großes Schauspielhaus and the

French and German cathedrals, and before reunification was used by the SED, the official party of the former East Germany, as a training centre. To the rear is an architectural icon of the new Berlin, the Galéries Lafayette department store designed by Jean Nouvel, while its immediate neighbour on the corner is another hotel, the Four Seasons, in a building designed by Josef Paul Kleihues.

The existing structure was completely gutted, but its heavy, ornate character – typical of Berlin's socialist legacy – made it hard for the interior designers to make something special for Dorint. But Harald Klein, whose creations include the Arabella Sheraton Pelikan in Hanover, and his partner Bert Haller took on the challenge with composure. 'Our goal is to create generous and sensual spaces with clear structures,' they explain. 'Our guests will find what they want in a contemporary environment: luxury, intimacy and comfort without vulgarity or ostentation.' The very narrow entrance to the building means that first impressions are necessarily low key. This applies also to the modest reception area. Only on the mezzanine floor, where the tables of the Atrium café are set out under huge lampshades, does the airy and spacious character of the building become apparent. For gourmet dining at street level there is Restaurant Aigner, which looks as if it is independent of the hotel. It has an Adolf-Loos-inspired interior that was transferred to Berlin in its original form from the historic Viennese café of the same name. The large health and fitness centre on the top storey of the hotel offers views over the centre of Berlin. For larger-scale conferences, the hotel has redeveloped another relic of East Germany in a neighbouring building: a former meeting room of the German Protestant church, preserved in its original form complete with stalactite chandeliers. The only new addition here is the underlit glass floor, which gives the space the feel of a stage-set.

above
A show only at night: glazed entrance to the neo-Art Nouveau building, now occupied by the Dorint Hotel.

opposite top
Atrium Café: spacious breakfast and dining area on the mezzanine level

opposite bottom
Check-in counter: reception with adjoining lobby seating

left
Prominent neighbourhood: the hotel is located opposite Schinkel's classicist theatre buidling and shares a block with Jean Nouvel's Galéries Lafayette department store.

next spread
Staging conferences: the old meeting hall of a former Protestant church serves today as the conference centre. The original interior was restored and a new underlit glass floor added.

right
Skillful intervention:
the new central staircase
and graphic windows
open up the old
unfavourable spaces.

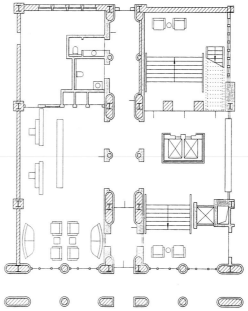

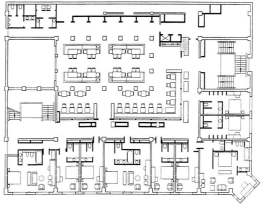

Small is beautiful:
the layout of the standard
bathrooms is very
economical. The wash
basins face a glass
wall, on the other side
of the guest room.

above
**Floor plans of ground floor
(top) and first floor (bottom).**

left
**Stepping out: only a few
of the rooms have
access to balconies above
an inner courtyard.**

THE New York architect Rafael Vinoly has extensive experience in both large- and small-scale building projects. He was born in Uruguay and worked in Argentina until 1978, emigrating after the military dictatorship took power there. In the mid-1990s he lived mostly in the Far East, while his biggest building to date, the Tokyo International Forum, was taking shape. Immediately after completing that tour de force, he started work on designs for the refurbishment of the Roger Williams Hotel in Manhattan.

The building, dating from 1928 and located at the less desirable end of Madison Avenue, had deteriorated into little more than a down-at-heel dosshouse. The property had been discovered by Gotham Hospitality Group, who saw it as a 'turnaround case' offering immense redevelopment potential. This group had already written a new chapter in New York hotel history with other regeneration projects such as the Mansfield and the Shoreham; the Roger Williams, which opened in 1997, was another addition to their list of success stories.

Vinoly adopted a clear strategy for the project: 'You need to start with what is already there. The important thing is not to contradict the nature of the building. If you concentrate on a couple of very simple notions, and carry them through, you achieve quite a lot and even gain a certain sophistication in the way that the various pieces are put together.' He opened up the original façade by adding large windows, more than 6 metres (20 feet) high,

reaching from the floor to the ceiling of the lobby. A number of guest rooms had to be sacrificed in order to create this impressively spacious foyer, and a gallery was created for the mezzanine lounge above the reception area. Three fluted, zinc-clad pillars provide a focal point in the entrance hall. Warm, honey-coloured maple is used extensively in both the public areas and the 202 guest rooms.

Vinoly also designed a good deal of the furniture in the hotel. The underlying principle of all the interior designs was a skilful reinterpretation of contemporary pared-down Japanese style. Only the art works refer back to the former splendour of the Roger Williams: the four statues in the lobby and almost 300 prints spread throughout the hotel all date from the 1930s. The extensive *Sports et Divertissements* series created by Charles Martin after compositions by Eric Satie enlivens the corridors on the guest floors. Each corridor has its own theme – sailing, skiing, dancing, and so on.

In keeping with the usual practice at modern business hotels, the establishment does not have its own restaurant (except for a breakfast room). A neighbouring restaurant, Mad 28, supplies meals for guests who wish to dine in their rooms.

above
Corner position: the entrance to the Roger Williams, as well as all of the 6 metre (20 foot) high ground-floor windows, were newly cut into the old façade.

opposite
Colossal style: giant zinc-clad pillars dominate the lobby and make a perfect setting for the grand piano.

below left
Ground-floor plan.

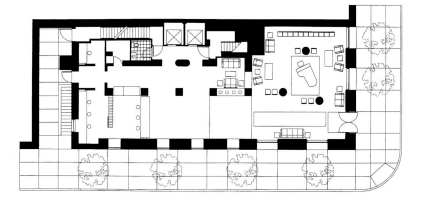

opposite
Two-level lobby: view of the reception desk, which is situated below the breakfast mezzanine.

above
Goddesses from the 1930s: four statues line the reception area.

left
Honey room: plain maple gives the guest rooms a feeling of warm domestic elegance.

Great Eastern Hotel

London, UK	Architecture: The Manser Practice
2000	Interior design: Conran & Partners

THE great metropolitan railway stations were once the gateways to the rest of the world. Many of them also offered well-heeled travellers luxurious hotel accommodation. An example of this was the Great Eastern Hotel in London's Liverpool Street station, which opened in 1884 and was extensively expanded in 1899–1901. By the second half of the 20th century the hotel was long past its best – but in London, the unsung capital of contemporary hotel design, it was more or less inevitable that an investor would appear on the scene to fill the historic building with new life and new style.

In 1996, the commission for the refurbishment of the

Great Eastern was entrusted to the Manser Practice, who had made a name for themselves in 1990 with an airy hotel hangar at London's Heathrow airport (now the Hilton). With one radical intervention they solved the main problem of the existing structure – the lack of an impressive lobby – by creating a six-storey-high atrium within the larger wing of the building, on Bishopsgate, to house the entrance and the reception area. The guest accommodation that had been sacrificed to this architectural tour de force was replaced by the addition of three attic storeys – indeed, the number of rooms was increased by more than 100, to a total of 267.

The venerable firm of Conran & Partners were asked to redesign the interior of the new Great Eastern, and they showed that experience does not necessarily involve the repetition of tried and trusted models, but can, as in this case, provide a foundation for innovative design solutions. This is especially apparent in the catering facilities, four restaurants and three bars, all of which open directly onto the street, allowing them to operate and attract customers independently of the hotel. The main restaurant, the Aurora – covered by a beautifully restored glass dome dating from 1884 – can now be accessed from the Great Eastern's former entrance on Liverpool Street; next door is the entrance to the Terminus bistro. More restaurants are sited on the corners of the hotel's other wing.

Manser and Conran paid great attention to detail in the renovation of the Great Eastern, which cost a total of £65 million. The modern additions serve as an almost reverential backdrop to the old building, transforming it into an artistic exhibit, a historical document. This celebration of one of the glories of the railway's golden age was inspired by thoroughly patriotic motives, as Conran & Partners explain: 'The fundamental concept for the Great Eastern has been to produce a truly British design statement; a functional and contemporary identity for the hotel attuned to the practical needs of travellers whilst maintaining a sense of the drama and to some extent glamour inherent in the original building.'

left
Regained glory: new cantilevered entrance to the old Liverpool Street Station hotel.

opposite
Inner spiral: a spectacular void opens up from the new reception hall to the rooftop of the enlarged building.

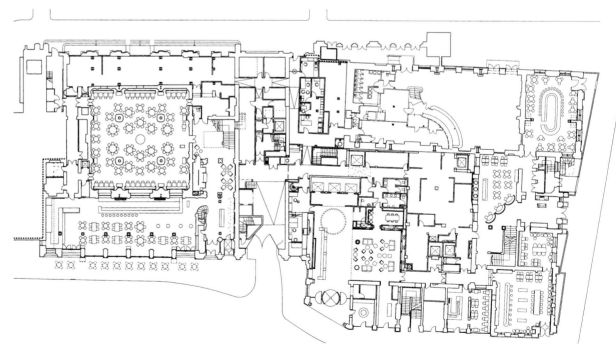

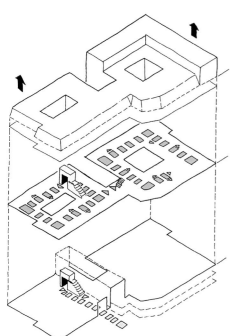

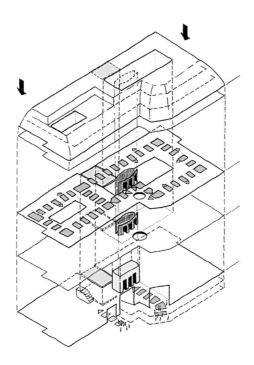

opposite top
Reversed façade: to the rear of the Great Eastern, a new inner courtyard was created, with rooms facing into the atrium space.

opposite bottom
Sketch of the ground floor, with the Aurora restaurant to the left and the new lobby space plus catering and conference facilities to the right.

above left
Domed dining: the restored Aurora restaurant is the gem of the revamped Great Eastern.

above
Looking in: standard guest room with window onto the atrium.

left
Expansion: the room capacity was enlarged by adding a new roofscape.

grand hotels

One of the welcome side-effects of the continuing boom in the international luxury hotel industry is the fact that the traditional genre of the 'grand hotel', which had long been regarded as moribund, is celebrating a renaissance. Top-quality, medium-sized hotels are beginning to pay again. In the right location a five-star hotel can offer a better return than an office building. As a result, a grand hotel such as the Kämp in Helsinki – alienated for decades from its original purpose, as a bank's head office – has been magnificently re-converted and expanded in keeping with its original style; and even the venerable Merchant's Exchange in New York has been transformed into the top hotel on Wall Street. The desire for unbridled luxury is growing and the highest hotel in the world, in the skyscraping architectural symbol of the new Shanghai, is an unmistakable descendant of these traditional flagship hotels, reinterpreting their spirit with an emphatically contemporary decor.

lust de luxe

Grand Hyatt, Shanghai

Shanghai, China 1999	Architecture: Skidmore, Owings & Merrill Interior design: Bilkey Llinas Design; Bregman & Hamann Architects; Dennis Reedy Design Consultants

CHINA'S equivalent of Manhattan is appearing on the banks of the Huangpu river. Over the past ten years, beyond the old centre of Shanghai, the ultra-modern giant office blocks of the new financial district of Pudong have been rising up out of the ground. Work on the Shanghai World Financial Center was temporarily halted during the Asian financial crisis; at a height of over 460 metres (1,510 feet) this skyscraper will eventually be the world's tallest. Until then, the Jin Mao Tower, completed in 1999 – the first building on this scale completed in the People's Republic – remains China's tallest building to date, at about 420 metres (1,380 feet). As for all other Pudong projects, the developer is the state itself, in this case the Foreign Trade Ministry.

The international competition for the Jin Mao Tower project was won by US-based architects Skidmore, Owings & Merrill. Their earthquake- and typhoon-proof design, which tapers at stepped intervals as it rises into the sky, supposedly refers to the Chinese pagoda style, but is in fact more reminiscent of the American Art Deco skyscrapers of the 1920s and 1930s. Behind the façade – made of steel, glass and aluminium – the building offers 278,000 metres (2,992,000 square feet) of gross floorspace on 88 floors. With its shopping arcades and cinemas and its conference and exhibition centre, the wide, six-storey base section has a very public feel. Office units are stacked above this, up to the 53rd storey – and on top of those is the Grand Hyatt Shanghai, the highest hotel in the world. The hotel's reception area, whose central atrium reaches right up to the 88th storey, is called Sky Lobby. In all, 555 rooms and suites and 12 restaurants and bars have been created to meet the needs of the hotel's guests – who certainly need to have a head for heights. A spectacular pool on the 57th storey, with windows all round it, blurs the boundaries between swimming and floating on air. Beneath the Observatory in the apex of the tower are two VIP Club floors with their own lounges. The interiors, created by a number of different design teams, radiate a modern, understated neutrality – out of character for the top category of the Hyatt chain, whose designs are

usually firmly rooted in conventional mainstream luxury. Apart from the Chinese Presidential Suite, scarcely any references to local culture are to be found. However, according to Skidmore, Owings & Merrill, the tower design follows traditional Chinese ideas: 'Jin Mao's design incorporates the Chinese lucky number eight in its height and derivation of setbacks. Each segment's height is reduced by one-eighth of the original base height and continues until the segment height is eight levels. At this point, the hotel begins and each segment reduces one-eighth of the eight-level segment, until it reaches the 88th level.'

In the absence of specific Chinese regulations, the architects applied US standards of safety for skyscrapers, adapting these to local needs, which included, for example, large and easily accessible shelter areas within the building. They devised a clever dual function to meet this requirement: on every 15th storey they included a conference floor which can be used as an evacuation space in the event of an emergency.

above
Chinese Manhattan: the towering skyline of the Shanghai river front, with the neo-Art Deco Grand Hyatt skyscraper on the right.

below left
Lobby to heaven: reception and lift area, from where guests ascend to the upper hotel storeys of the Jin Mao Tower.

above

Patio lounge: vivid flooring and wide windows characterize the luxurious lobby of the Grand Hyatt on the 56th floor.

left

Top spot: the Cloud 9 bar offers great views over downtown Shanghai. Structural elements turn into impressive interior features.

right
**Pool in the sky: the
opulent recreation deck is
located on the 57th floor.**

below
**Western comfort: the
standard rooms follow a
solid, conservative
occidental style.**

bottom
Lobby-level floor plan.

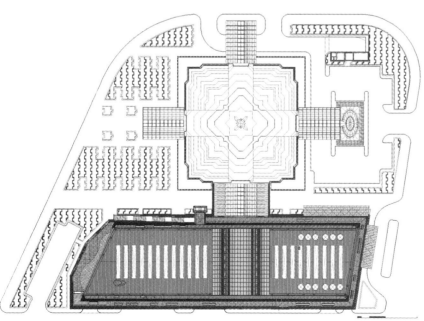

The Regent Wall Street

New York, USA 1999	Architecture: M/G Architects Interior design: Wilson & Associates; Hablinsky Interiors

'FINDING any property in New York is extremely difficult, and this building satisfied all our criteria. We had to have it,' explains Paul Hanley, the president of the luxury hotel chain Regent International. 'First, it has a great location. Second, it has outstanding architecture, inside and out, in a class by itself. Third, the structure, which is built around a courtyard on the upper floors, accommodates an extremely large guest room. You rarely find a conversion property with such a good floorplate.'

The building in question – 55 Wall Street – is one of the most important landmarks in New York City's financial district. It was at this address that the city's merchants established their trading exchange in 1827. When the Merchants' Exchange was destroyed in the great fire of 1835, the classical architect Isaiah Rogers replaced it with a much larger building, a magnificent construction with an Ionic colonnade occupying the whole block; for some years, this follow-up also housed the stock exchange. From 1863 to 1899 the New York Customs was based there (one of the customs inspectors, Herman Melville, rose to international fame as the author of Moby Dick). Then the National City Bank acquired the site as its headquarters and in 1907 the bank commissioned the architects McKim, Mead & White to design a colossal extension, adding five more storeys – which were fortunately concealed behind a double Corinthian colonnade. The bankers sold the property in 1990, since when it had stood pretty much empty until New York investors Sidney Kimmel and Richard

Butera came up with the idea of transforming the building into a luxury hotel. The purchase price was US $27.5 million, and the renovation, restoration and conversion absorbed twice as much again.

With 144 rooms and suites, the Regent Wall Street, which opened in late 1999, is small by the standards of New York's luxury hotels, but for sheer grandeur it beats the competition by miles. The impressive banking hall of 1907, lined in grey Botticini marble, with the largest Wedgwood frieze in the world around its majestic dome, is one of the most magnificent banqueting halls anywhere. The restaurant 55 Wall Street, situated behind the colonnade on the first storey – with an outdoor terrace for use in the warmer months – offers excellent front-row seats from which to observe the hurly-burly of the financial district. There is no better place for discreet negotiations than the conference room known as The Vault, the bank's former strong-room. Only one relic of the building's past has not yet been put to good use: in the cellar are four prison cells, which survive from the time when violations of customs regulations were punished by instant imprisonment.

above
The former Merchants' Exchange: the building is regarded as a major New York landmark.

opposite
Trading for guests: the hotel's Grand Ballroom was originally a banking hall. The dome is lined with the world's largest Wedgwood frieze.

above
The Regent Wall Street's majestic space is a perfect setting for large events.

right
Wall Street splash: a bath room at the downtown hotel.

left
Money is suite: one of the former trading exchange's guest rooms.

below
Meet in the vault: what was once the strong-room is now a favourite conference space for investors and corporate raiders.

Park Hyatt

Melbourne, Australia 1999	Architecture: Buchan Group Interior design: Tatron

THE address – 1 Parliament Square – tells you all you need to know about the location of the Park Hyatt. All around are the majestic government buildings of the state of Victoria; opposite is St Patrick's Cathedral, Melbourne's oldest church. The new H-shaped building, whose 12-storey central section towers over the two side wings, is a fine example of discreet postmodernist architecture that makes it a fitting addition to this upmarket neighbourhood. One of the first guests to stay there, soon after it opened, was President Jiang Zemin of China.

The Park Hyatt was a second excursion into the hotel business for local developer Max Moar, who has invested successfully in shopping centres and office complexes with his partner Ted Lustig over the past 25 years. As with the magnificent five-star Grand Hyatt in Melbourne's Collins Street (1985), Moar secured the top American chain as hotel operator. He awarded the interior design contract to the Tatron team from Palm Beach, Florida. The hotel cost a total of Aus $150 million to build and, although the outer shell does not exactly shout extravagance, the interior designers were allowed to go well over the top. As David Parsons, Director of Tatron, explains, 'Conceptually the Park Hyatt is a careful combination of romance, reflection and remembrance; it is a boutique hotel, but with a grand arts style. This is the catalyst for all the interior design issues. The hotel is like a jewelry box...which, when open, becomes your secret garden.' This poetic interpretation is accurate in some respects. Starting in the lobby, the visitor is greeted by a succession of elegant spatial solutions whose ornamental flourishes betray an almost obsessive attention to detail. The Art Deco style is rather strained in places and not always stylistically accurate. Its aberrations are similar to those in certain luxury hotels in Japan and other parts of Asia, although in most of those other hotels the interiors are a good deal less precious in their execution, and what looks fake is indeed fake; here the dazzling grandeur is entirely

genuine. With its 241 guest rooms and suites, the Park Hyatt may be the Grand Hyatt's junior in terms of size, but for sheer ostentation it surpasses the larger hotel by a long way.

The outstanding gems in the Park Hyatt box are the two restaurant areas: the Trilogy Bistro and Lounge, on two levels, and the Radi Restaurant and Bar, on five levels with an open kitchen at the centre. The circular ballroom is crowned by a 5.5 metre (18 foot) high silver dome. There are open fireplaces everywhere: in the reception, in the library (which has a collection of 7,000 books, most of them Australiana) and in most of the suites. The bathrooms are extremely luxurious – all of them have large waterproof television screens set into the wall.

The top storey of the building's central section is reserved for the Regency Club, an exclusive hotel-within-a-hotel for VIPs. Immediately below this – with panoramic views over the city, Port Philipp Bay and Treasury Gardens – is the Park Club Health and Day Spa, where guests can have their spirits soothed and their bodies pampered. The health and fitness facilities include a 25 metre (82 foot) swimming pool, lined with columns and with a vaulted ceiling above, and a full-sized tennis court on the outdoor deck. In another attempt to promote good health, the entire hotel, except for the Cuba cigar lounge, has been declared a smoke-free zone.

above
Late postmodernism: the Park Hyatt is an unobtrusive newcomer in the heart of Melbourne's governmental district.

opposite
Sweeping stairs and galleries: the entrance hall shows the design principle of the hotel's interiors: boldness with shiny materials and exaggerated decorative pattern.

Dining theatre: In the Radi restaurant, guests sit on multi-level balconies.

above
Subterranean swim:
pool area, flanked by
massive columns and
furnished with neo-
romanesque settees.

left
Waterproof tellies: in the guest bathrooms, built-in TV sets are the main innovative feature.

below
Trilogy restaurant: a club atmosphere and some communal tables form the hotel's second catering venue.

The Gleneagles Hotel

| Gleneagles, UK 1998 | Interior design: Sedley Place |

TEN years ago United Distillers dreamed up a plan to turn a famous old name into a luxury global brand. The company was part of the Guinness group and its portfolio included the legendary Perthshire hotel Gleneagles – whose name arguably had the potential to sell all kinds of luxury goods, from top-quality whisky to golf clothing and accessories. The commission to develop this potential was entrusted to London agency Sedley Place, who had been responsible for many of United Distillers' brand images and packaging designs. Following the merger of Guinness and Grand Met, the group embracing United Distillers is now called Diageo, and its core business is based on such household names as Smirnoff, Johnnie Walker, J&B, Gordon's, Häagen-Dazs and Burger King, to name just a few.

Sedley Place got down to work, but, unfortunately, the client at some stage lost interest in the project. Before the plans were consigned to the filing cabinet for ever, the Gleneagles management intervened in the belief that discarded designs for such trivia as notepaper and souvenirs might prove useful. In the event, using such remainders led to the refurbishment of all the main interiors at Gleneagles.

Mick Nash, Managing Director of Sedley Place, who was put in charge of the new interior design, defined the project as a classic brand repositioning: 'The new Gleneagles identity consists of three interlocking schemes: corporate marks and signs, the style of furniture and fittings, and the integrated use of pattern. This identity embraces not only the way in which Gleneagles presents itself through promotion and advertising but also the way in which the rooms are styled and furnished, right through to the fabric of the building itself.' The real challenge was to revive past glories without drowning in nostalgia.

The Caledonian Railway company had built Gleneagles in 1924 as a luxury hotel with a railway station, and until the 1950s this 'Riviera of the Highlands', set in grounds of 350 hectares, was a seasonal port of call for the British aristocracy, who went there for hunting and golf. The three 18-hole championship golf courses – King's, Queen's and

Monarch's – are still among the most famous in the world, but the hotel, with 229 rooms and suites, has had to battle to retain its prime position. Its success springs largely from the highly focused work by Sedley Place, whose refurbishment avoids cliché. Each of the public areas was tackled in turn: the bar, the reception area and the country club. The new designs are both varied and stylistically unified, drawing on an original design canon developed specially for the hotel – located between Art Deco and Art Nouveau, with some unmistakable borrowings from Charles Rennie Mackintosh.

The designers avoided using widely available furniture and light fittings: originality was their holy grail. As a result, the new Gleneagles has a highly individual character that embodies exclusivity – as befits the upmarket hideaway of one of the world's largest beverages and catering groups.

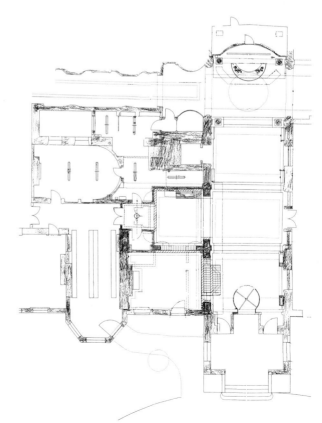

left
Ground-floor plan, with reception, lobby, bar and restaurant areas.

opposite top
New splendour: the Gleneagles bar, refurbished in a lavish Art Nouveau manner, looks more authentic than the original.

opposite bottom
Attention to detail: chandeliers and furniture were precisely crafted in the period style of the hotel's Golden Age.

above
Tribute to the master: the guest rooms reinterpret designs by the great Scottish architect Charles Rennie Mackintosh.

opposite top and bottom
Not your average country club: the pool house features colourful tents and seating under palm trees. Witty yellow umbrellas surround the shower heads.

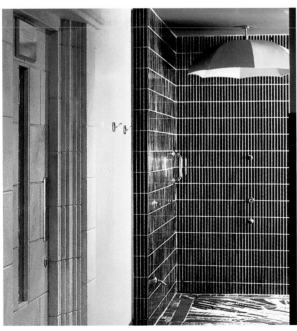

Hotel Kämp

Helsinki, Finland
1999

Architecture/Interior design: EAA International

IT was in 1887, during the first golden age of the European grand hotels, when restaurateur Carl Wilhelm Kämp opened his luxury establishment in the Finnish capital. This five-storey hotel by architect Theodor Höijer (to which a further storey was added in 1915), set in a prominent location on Esplanadi Park between the main railway station and cathedral square, remained a focal point of the city's social and political life for more than half a century.

When the hotel finally closed in the 1950s, its interior had suffered long-term neglect and its wooden foundations were threatened by rot. After a long tussle with the heritage preservation bodies, the owner of the property, Kansallis Bank of Finland, obtained permission to demolish the old building and create a new office block, while preserving the main façade and a few parts of the interior. This project was duly completed in 1969. Thirty years later, a wave of mergers in the international finance sector made it possible for the legendary Hotel Kämp to rise from the ashes. The property's owners, the newly formed Merita Bank, put the building on the market again as a hotel. The Starwood Group of America was awarded the contract as hotel operator, adding the Kämp to its high-class Luxury Collection chain, which includes the Danieli in Venice and the Imperial in Vienna.

The London-based interior designers EAA International – who had already produced successful designs for luxury hotels such as the Adlon in Berlin and Istanbul's Çiragan Palace – were entrusted with the complete reconstruction of the building. For EAA's director, Ezra Attia, the designers' sole guiding principle was to recapture the building's original splendour as faithfully as possible: 'The aim was for the interiors of the new Hotel Kämp to encapsulate the spirit of the grand hotel of the past, and the essence of the original hotel in particular. It was equally important to ensure that the amenities demanded by both business and leisure travellers at the end of the 20th century were sensitively introduced.'

The task was to unify the building's three disparate sections – the remnants of the original structure, the

1960s office block and a new hotel wing – in a harmonious whole incorporating 179 rooms and suites, while maintaining an authentic historical feel. The designers studied archive documents and photos as a basis for their interpretative tour de force. The newly constructed entrance hall, which functions as a linchpin between the three hotel buildings, shows how brilliantly the interior design strategy succeeded. In contrast with what happened at the Adlon in Berlin, where ill-judged compromises diminished the impact of the lobby design, at the Hotel Kämp the original stylistic motifs were copied exactly and the building's grand historic proportions were respected. The transitions between old and new appear entirely organic, and the restoration of the surviving public areas – including the former reception hall, the large Kämp restaurant and the impressive Hall of Mirrors – display a loving attention to detail.

Finland's history is evident everywhere you go in the new Kämp. The function rooms are named after famous Finnish figures such as the architect Eliel Saarinen, the composer Jean Sibelius and the athletics star Paavo Nurmi. The Presidential Suite, measuring 258 square metres (2,780 square feet), is named after General and President Baron Gustav Mannerheim. The Balance Club health suite is also designed in typically Finnish fashion, and the steam rooms and Turkish baths can be booked for private use or for business meetings and other intimate gatherings.

above left
A hospitality landmark: the famous Helsinki Hotel has been a bank head office for nearly five decades.

opposite
The spirit of 1887: the Mirror Room is one of the few original interiors that has been preserved, and now restored to its former glory.

opposite
Faithful to the past: the design of the new entrance hall follows historical patterns. The lobby space serves as the hub for three different buildings that form the hotel.

left
Meet the original: the lounge in the oldest part of the hotel.

below left
Ground floor plan.

below right
Fin-de-siècle **indulgence: guest-room interiors are rich recreations of classical luxury.**

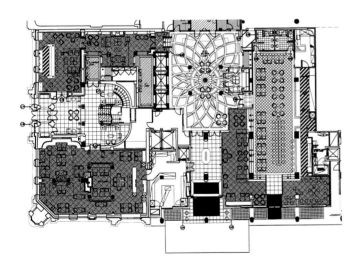

resort & entertainment hotels

In the cosmos, black holes are where the concentration of matter is at its highest. Anything that gets too close to them is sucked inside, into a dimension of nothingness that is absolute density. The principle behind the megalomaniac entertainment resorts works in a very similar way. These glittering worlds of fun accumulate artificial attractions from all over the globe, transform them into a mass of nothingness – and generate phenomenal revenues from a combination of entertainment and gambling. The Las Vegas principle operates well beyond the Nevada desert. Even the former pirate coast of Dubai – transformed into a display of fairytale splendour, with no expense spared – can claim a place on the map of luxury destinations. But there are alternatives to these phantasmagorias, impressive as they are. This is demonstrated by holiday resorts which combine scale with thoughtfulness, adapt to their natural surroundings, and follow minimally invasive ecological strategies heralding an alternative, gentler type of tourism – which does not involve the sacrifice of habitual comforts and popular entertainments.

worlds of fun

Burj al Arab

Dubai	Architecture: W.S. Atkins
United Arab Emirates	Interior design: Khuan Chew Associates
2000	

IN what has turned out to be the most ambitious and expensive tourist project of modern times, the emirate of Dubai has created, within a period of just five years, the centrepiece of the 'Arabian Riviera' – a glittering complex of spectacular luxury hotels, a leisure park and a marina, on a coast once infested with pirates. A well-focused infrastructure strategy has transformed this small desert state into the Hong Kong of the Middle East. Today only a third of Dubai's gross domestic product is derived from oil. The state is now looking to the expanding global travel market to provide increasing income, and the Ministry of Economy and Tourism has launched a major offensive.

The most important natural attributes of any holiday paradise – sand, sun and sea – were already present in Dubai in abundance, and the location meant that the architecture could not fail to be influenced by the fairytale world of the *Arabian Nights*. The huge, prestigious project on Jumeirah Beach – conveniently located near the capital and the international airport – was designed and carried out from 1994 onwards by the British architects W.S. Atkins. The bold concrete wave of five-star Jumeirah Beach Hotel, with its 600 rooms and suites and offshore marina, opened in 1997. Soon after this the Wild Wadi theme park with two dozen water adventure rides was completed and the first of the 19 guest villas in the exclusive Beit Al Bahar complex, belonging to Jumeirah Beach Hotel, were ready for occupation. In autumn 1999, the project culminated in the

building of Burj al Arab, the Arabian Tower.

Set in splendid isolation on an artificial island 280 metres (920 feet) off the coast, Burj al Arab stands on 250 foundation pillars and is 321 metres (1,050 feet) in height. According to W.S. Atkins, 'The proposals broke new ground in design and technology, with a tower shaped like a billowing sail, reminiscent of an Arabic dhow, erected on a triangular island. The aim was to create a hotel that would not just offer an unparalleled level of luxury and service but also become an icon for Dubai.'

The two glazed guest wings, which look as if they are suspended in the bold curves of the outer structure, form the sides of a narrow triangle which is completed on the land end by the largest textile façade covering ever constructed. The helicopter platform, which juts out daringly from the building, and even more so the Al Muntaha sky restaurant, suspended at a height of almost 198 metres, look like virtual-world creations from a science-fiction film. At night the real marvels begin, when the giant teflon-covered façade begins to glow in myriad colours and the towers of flames around the fountains blaze in front of the hotel entrance.

The project's interior designers, Khuan Chew Associates (who also worked on Jumeirah Beach Hotel), did not have to count their pennies. They used nearly 3,000 square metres (32,300 square feet) of gold leaf to decorate the public areas and the 202 suites (spread over two storeys). Oriental grandeur and luxury kitsch have scarcely ever been combined in more audacious fashion. The same showy excess prevails everywhere – but the result is great fun, and a veritable feast for the eyes. Burj al Arab also has some surprises in store: for example, guests are transported to their table at the Al Mahara fish restaurant by submarine, enjoying a three-minute journey through a marine wonderland before sitting down for their meal.

above
Arabian fantasies come true: the Burj al Arab skyscraper is built on an artificial island off the Dubai coast.

left
Underwater wonders: guests in the restaurant are surrounded by a giant aquarium.

next spread
Middle Eastern delights: relaxation area, decorated in a neo-pharaonic style, with splash pool.

above
Nothing but suites: all guest units are two-level suites. Bathrooms feature marble and gold taps; bedrooms are equipped with extravagant canopy beds.

opposite
Breathtaking welcome: in the atrium, the protruding forms of the guest-room wings rise up to the sky.

Couran Cove Island Resort

South Stradbroke Island, Australia 1998	Architecture/Interior design: Daryl Jackson

REGARDED as one of the greatest long-distance runners of all time, the Australian sporting idol Ron Clarke set 17 world records, but during a top-class career that lasted from 1963 to 1970 he never won an Olympic gold medal. Perhaps Clarke took some wry satisfaction from the fact that teams from Switzerland, Germany and Norway established their training quarters for the 2000 Olympics in a place where he has since recorded a top-class achievement of a very different sort – as the instigator of what is probably the largest eco-tourism project, not only in the Australian continent, but also in the world beyond.

Located on South Stradbroke Island, off the coast of Queensland, the Couran Cove Island Resort – which covers 252 hectares (622 acres) and borders 25 kilometres (16 miles) of beach – can accommodate up to 1,200 guests, but the contrast between Couran Cove and the nearby Gold Coast, lined with high-density tourist tower blocks, could hardly be more striking. On the sandy island, with its mangroves and rainforest, strict eco-friendly principles are in force – and the plan for the resort, conceived by architect Daryl Jackson, had to conform to these principles in every way. 'All the buildings are designed to convey an attitude towards and for the landscape, to infiltrate the bush, to hover over the water. This is regional maritime architecture at its best. Couran Cove is distinguished by the fact that the eco-system of habitat and humans remains largely intact. The keys to achieving this were retaining trees where possible, careful use of materials, and protection of the dunes and forest. These are relatively new for tourist projects, yet sustainability is one of the lessons the Australian landscape can offer.'

The reception building, restaurants and apartment buildings (192 apartments and 25 villas, most of them on stilts and jutting out over the water) are all made of wood, with corrugated-metal roofs, and loosely grouped around a natural bay and inland lagoon. In the middle of the lagoon is Spa Island, with bathing facilities that include a heated 25 metre (82 foot) swimming pool with ten lanes. Hidden in the surrounding dunes and bush are a further 50 'nature resort' cabins. All the guest quarters are equipped with kitchenettes, and groceries can be delivered to order, for no extra charge, from the resort's general store. Guests can keep track of their water, electricity and gas consumption via the television monitors in their rooms.

Practical considerations apart, Couran Cove is a place devoted to pleasure. It aims to provide guests with a fun-filled holiday in a natural setting. The sports centre offers just about every athletic pursuit imaginable. You can do long jump, high jump or trampolining, clamber up a rock face, play basketball, baseball, tennis, squash, bowls, boules or golf – the tartan track is 100 metres (328 feet) long, with an electronic timing system. There are also two fully equipped fitness centres, one indoors and the other outdoors.

In both ecological and sporting terms, Couran Cove is way ahead of the competition. Best of all is the fact that the design of this leisure world is an uncompromising celebration of contemporary aesthetics. The result is an architecture that is clear, simple and modern – and all the better for avoiding any fake exoticism or Robinson Crusoe-style nostalgia.

below left
Huge, but not oppressive: Daryl Jackson's architectural design nestles well into the natural landscape of the island.

opposite top
Hovering over the water: guest apartments are grouped in low-rise wings around a lagoon.

opposite bottom
Plain and inviting: the interiors of the guest units are designed in an uncompromising modern style, offering all contemporary comfort.

above
Hidden in the bush: additional guest cabins are located in the dense vegetation of South Stradbroke Island.

above right
View from the hotel arrival breezeway into the former general store, now the Boardwalk Bar and Café.

The Venetian

Las Vegas, USA	Architecture: Wimberley Allison Tong & Goo;
1999	TSA of Nevada
	Interior design: Dougall Design; Wilson & Associates

THE billionaire Sheldon G. Adelson made his fortune in many different businesses, including Comdex, the biggest computer fair in the USA. His property portfolio in the gambling paradise of Las Vegas included the legendary casino hotel Sands, which at 40 years old was positively ancient by local standards. In 1996 he razed the building to the ground to make way for a glamorous project that set new records even among the many gigantic creations in this gaming metropolis. The idea came from Adelson's second wife, with whom he had honeymooned in Venice. The Venetian hotel was intended to represent nothing less than a condensed version of that splendid Italian city. The project would cost billions, but Adelson planned to capitalize on the combination of the existing trade fair and conference venue The Sands Expo – now extended to 150,000 square metres (1,614,000 square feet) – with the new hotel and entertainment complex, which would be built in two stages. One of the maxims for the project architects Wimberley Allison Tong & Goo was to be different from the competition, as they explain: 'The design of the entire resort challenges the traditional Las Vegas hotel template which works to keep guests inside the casino for as long as possible.'

The Venetian is the first all-suite hotel on the Las Vegas Strip. The 35-storey tower block with its three wings has a total of 3,036 room units, each covering an average of 65 square metres (700 square feet) with a marble entrance, lower-level living area and luxury bathroom.

The second tower construction, The Venetian Isle of Lido, completed in 2001, doubled the hotel's capacity. The result was the largest integrated trade fair, congress and hotel complex in the USA, created at a cost of nearly US $3 billion – complete with full-size replicas of the Doge's Palace, the Campanile and the Ca D'Oro, and a Rialto Bridge with a moving walkway leading to the car park. St Mark's Square and the Grand Canal – with electrically powered gondolas and a wave machine, but with genuine singing gondolieri – form the backdrop for the shopping mall, covered by a permanently sunny artificial sky, whose dimensions utterly eclipse the former frontrunner (the Forum Shops at Caesar's Palace). Other attractions include the roof garden, with its five swimming pools and the Canyon Ranch Spa Club, two theatres and a branch of London's Madame Tussaud's waxworks.

Adelson decided that this array of entertainment venues should be balanced by the presence of great art, so he built not one but two Nevada branches of the Guggenheim museum, designed by avant-garde architect Rem Koolhaas. In the lobby a 700 square metre (7,530 square foot) box of corroded steel provides a setting for temporary displays from the Guggenheim and the Hermitage in St Petersburg, and outside there is an austere 6,000 square metre (64,560 square foot) art gallery for the permanent exhibition. Adelson's aim was to outdo his local competitor, Stephen A. Wynn. The latter's nearby fantasy hotel Bellagio boasted genuine Picassos and Renoirs – until financial problems forced him to sell his Las Vegas empire and the new owner, the MGM Grand Group, owned by Kirk Kerkorian, rapidly converted parts of the impressive art collection to cash.

opposite
Façade of one of the biggest convention facilities in the USA. Replicated Venetian glories, like the Doge's Palace, are the attractions of this integrated trade, congress and hotel casino complex.

below left
Cross-section showing entry to the casino and the Grand Canal Shoppes mall level.

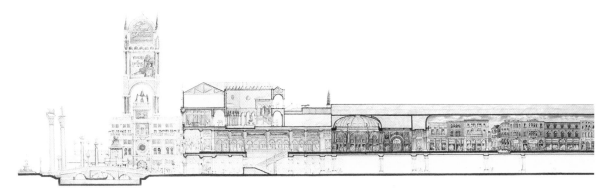

above
Crossing the Canal: a
bridge over the indoor
stretch of water is also a
retail area.

right
Palatial reception:
registration lobby facing
gallery to the casino, with
Italian marble flooring.

far right
Gondola experience: under
the artificial sky of the
indoor mall, guests can
enjoy a boat ride,
complete with singing
gondolier.

Paris

Las Vegas, USA 1999	Architecture: Bergman, Walls & Youngblood Interior design: Yates-Silverman; Kovacs & Associates

NOT so long ago Americans would set off across the Atlantic to 'do' Europe, sampling the wonders of its major cities in the space of a few days. Now tourists from all over the world flock to Las Vegas to gape at replicas of famous cities, re-created along the Strip, whose buildings are in fact no more than façades for innumerable casinos and thousands of hotel rooms piled one on top of another. This formula has been in use for some time in Las Vegas, in classical-style fantasy temples such as Caesar's Palace and the Luxor. Then in 1993 came the first attempt at a sterilized, downsized postcard panorama cityscape with the mega-hotel New York New York. Paris, which opened in 1999 and cost US $795 million to build, is a prominent new arrival on this scene.

The local architects Bergman, Walls & Youngblood showed great care in their task of copying and reducing, as their director Joel Bergman explains: 'We took every step possible to see that the reproductions were designed and built with architectural integrity and authenticity. The city of Paris has a special place in people's hearts and we wanted to make sure that these re-creations brought people to the Paris they remember or have always envisioned.'

In some cases the architects even consulted the original plans, for example when creating their 1:50 version of the Eiffel Tower – which, at more than 160 metres (525 feet) tall, is hardly pint-sized (and even higher than the real Cologne Cathedral). The imitation, like the original, has a panoramic restaurant and a viewing platform right at the top. Visitors generally have to queue, too, although people waiting in line in Las Vegas at least get to stand on Pont Alexandre III, which is mounted as a footbridge below the casino ceiling, high above the cacophony of games machines. Other replica Parisian landmarks are the Arc de Triomphe, two thirds its original size, in front of the main entrance; the Opéra Garnier, as the outer shell for the theatre, accommodating 1,200 spectators; the Galérie des Glaces from Versailles, as a foyer for the Champagne Ball Room which covers nearly 8,000 square metres (86,000 square feet) (it was the largest in Las Vegas when it opened); Place des Vosges, downgraded to a forecourt for the China restaurant; and Montmartre, as part of the indoor shopping mall. Even the massive, angled block which houses the 2,961 rooms and suites is supposedly modelled on a historical original: the Parisian Hôtel de Ville, inflated into a 34-storey stretch version. Yet this is where profit-driven distortion finally ousts any notion of faithfulness to the original and imitation architecture becomes the icing on a cheap and sickly cake.

left
Intriguing the eyes: inner façades, citing old Paris, frame the reception area.

right
Shrunken, but still glorious: Paris landmarks, like the Eiffel Tower, were replicated in 1:50 scale for the Las Vegas casino hotel.

above right
Three-dimensional postcards: the catering mile of Paris Las Vegas features everything from Métro canopies to marble monuments.

right
Boudoir feeling: guest room, decorated in fake Louis-XV style.

Just married: the wedding chapel, complete with period chandeliers and angelic frescoes.

Sheraton Miramar Resort Hotel

El Gouna, Egypt 1997	Architecture: Michael Graves & Associates; Rami El Dahan, Soheir Farid Interior design: Michael Graves & Associates

MICHAEL Graves, the grand master of postmodernism, had long been fascinated by the land of the pharaohs. A number of his highly imaginative hotel projects in the USA, in particular, carry echoes of ancient Egyptian style. However, in spite of these elements of his work, it was the monumental pyramid feature of Graves's Swan (1989) at Disney World in Florida that prompted the Egyptian property developer Samih Sawiris to give the Princeton professor of architecture his first commission in the Middle East. On a 150,000 square metre (1,614,000 square foot) sandspit in the Red Sea, Graves has created a leisure complex incorporating canals and surrounded by beaches and an artificial lagoon. By day, it is an incredibly colourful and varied sight in the shimmering sunlight; at night, it shines like a fairytale city from the *Arabian Nights.*

Generally, tourists arriving from the colder reaches of Europe for a fortnight in the Egyptian sun are not hard to please. The nondescript Arabian-style architecture that is so common everywhere from Turkey to Tunisia would most probably have been sufficient here, too. But such architecture would not have required the involvement of Michael Graves.

Graves manages to embody in the Sheraton Miramar Resort both the spirit of the place and his own delight at discovery, as well as incorporating elements of traditional style and local crafts. The project sensitively blends local architectural features with quotations from the architect's treasure trove of classical motifs, and one searches in vain for the gaudy plagiarism of ancient splendours evident in Hollywood B movies. Graves responds to the scale of the site as a whole with brilliant variations on typological models. He packs the rooms and suites – more than 400 of them, all overlooking the water – behind a succession of one- to three-storey façades, with roofs modelled to domes, barrel vaulting or lanterns.

To give this artificial oasis a feel of authentic spontaneity, the rooms – made entirely in the traditional way, using bricks without concrete reinforcement – have been left mainly unplastered on the inside. Graves also designed all the interiors, and the fittings and furniture were produced locally rather than abroad: 'We have tried to be sympathetic to the constructional possibilities and vernacular methods, which has led to interesting links with the local character and context. Although the furniture we have designed is not explicitly Egyptian, its "rustic" character leads to a quality that is both archaic and vernacular.'

The Sheraton Miramar Resort is a pilot project for the planned expansion of El Gouna as a tourist centre. Further stages of development are under way, and the local investor has made the only possible choice by entrusting the design work to Michael Graves.

below
Fata Morgana for real: the shoreline of the Miramar resort was built to a vernacular architectural typology.

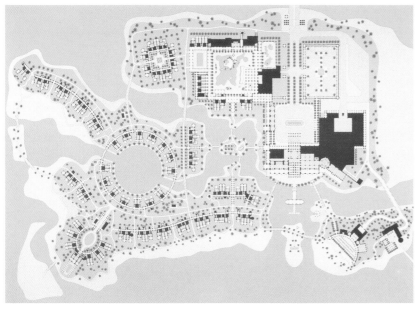

above
**Sunseeker's paradise:
main pool area, with
domed guest apartments
in the background.**

left
**Site plan of the resort
complex.**

opposite
Illuminated spirits: behind
the bar counter, bottles
are kept in backlit, arched
niches.

above left
A touch of Graves: the
American postmodernist
also designed all the
interior features, including
the guest rooms.

above
Cool and cosy oasis:
main lobby of
the Miramar resort.

House of Blues Hotel

Chicago, USA 1998	Architecture: VQA Interior design: Cheryl Rowley

THE twin towers of Marina City, built between 1959 and 1964, symbolize the golden age of Chicago's second high-rise boom, when the city on Lake Michigan vied with New York to become the skyscraper capital of the world. Marina City incorporated an office block and a range of public amenities including a theatre, shops, restaurants and sports facilities, and for the architect Bertrand Goldberg the 60-storey cylindrical towers at the heart of Chicago's Loop district offered a model for a new unity between residential and working accommodation in America's decaying inner cities. But these towers – the tallest residential and concrete structures in the world at the time they were built – subsequently fell upon hard times. By the early 1990s, large parts of the site had become bankruptcy estate, and a major regeneration drive was required to bring new life to this important part of Chicago's fabric.

To the rescue came a foundation dedicated to the memory of a very different aspect of the city's heritage: the House of Blues organization, founded by Isaac Tigrets, which operates music clubs and restaurants throughout the USA, using its profits to fund charitable projects on behalf of race relations and education. The House of Blues, in partnership with Japanese investors, acquired the crisis-ridden property – in the city that is the traditional home of jazz and blues – and opened its most ambitious project to date in Marina City in 1998: the House of Blues Hotel, located in the former 16-storey office tower. The 367-room hotel is operated by the US-based Loews group. Its immediate neighbours include the Live Music Hall and Restaurant, a range of other restaurant outlets, the AMF Bowling Center and the Crunch health and fitness club; the new owners even spruced up the old landing stage on the lakeside.

The Californian interior designer Cheryl Rowley devised an exotic/nostalgic character for the hotel that incorporates elements of neo-Gothicism, Arabian-style romanticism,

Indian Maharajah-style magnificence and folk traditions of the southern US. In the lobby, Indian temple windows, Moroccan wall hangings, treasures from old sailing ships and golden Buddha statues form a prelude to the centrally placed sculpture by Walter Arnold: four powerful sandstone caryatid figures bearing a red and yellow canopy – their bodies have a Far Eastern appearance, while their heads draw on folk traditions of the US South.

This eclectic style is also apparent on the guest floors, some of which are designed to suit the requirements of particular groups. On the executive class level on the 14th storey, where guests have their own private lounge, the décor is elaborate and sophisticated; by contrast, the cabin-rooms storey offers all the usual facilities in half-sized rooms at a budget price. When guests check in, they are given their key cards and useful information in a CD box, accompanied by a free disc with music of their choice. The staff, dressed in jeans or chinos, wear backstage passes instead of name badges. Recordings of House of Blues concerts are played on the many TV monitors around the hotel. Guests can hang 'Don't bother me' signs on their doors if they wish to avoid being disturbed. And in the Blues Brothers Suite – covering nearly 170 square metres (1,830 square feet) – they can admire the original suits of the film stars John Belushi and Dan Ackroyd displayed in glass cases.

below
Giants from the South: the
focal point of the hotel
lobby is a sculpture by
Walter Arnold — four
sandstone caryatides,
holding the domed ceiling.

opposite
Prominent site: the House
of Blues Hotel is located in
the Marina City complex,
one of Chicago's finest
examples of 20th-century
modernism.

left, above and opposite
Eclectic mix: guest rooms offer a bridging of cultures and styles. The result is rather conventional and does not engage too much with the musical theme of the House of Blues Hotel.

House of Blues 165

Atlantis

Paradise Island, Bahamas 1998	Architecture: Wimberley Allison Tong & Goo Interior design: Wilson & Associates

SOL Kerzner, the head of the casino and hotel group Sun International, has always been a gifted storyteller, bringing his tales to life in the form of fantastic architectural creations. For Sun City, the gambling utopia he founded in South Africa in the early 1990s, he invented the kingdom of Lost City, constructing its mythical palace amid an adventure landscape that incorporated a water funfair and a manmade jungle.

Shortly after this, Kerzner went in search of Atlantis – and ended up building the sunken metropolis himself, on Paradise Island, off Nassau in the Bahamas. This myth-crazy Midas invested more than US $850 million in two stages, and following the completion of Royal Towers, the 23-storey main wing, the facilities offered by this gigantic resort complex can be summarized as follows: 2,327 rooms and suites; 38 restaurants, lounges and bars; the world's biggest artificial lagoon; half a dozen pools, plus a Maya pyramid with five water chutes – two of the transparent tubes lead right through the shark pool – and a subterranean archaeological maze called The Dig. More conventional features include a yacht marina, extensive events and conference facilities, and the obligatory casino.

What is particularly likeable about Kerzner's megalomaniac creations is that, unlike their conventional Las Vegas-style competitors, they do deliver on some of their visual promises. Getting guests to spend their money on gaming is not the sole and primary intention of Atlantis; it is also designed to provide a fulfilling holiday experience. 'Basically Atlantis is a series of integrated resorts and all guests have the adventure of moving through the totality of it, to discover some or all of what it has to offer,' says Sol

Kerzner. 'That's our secret, if you like. I've always believed in creating projects that will blow people away.'

For this project, Kerzner called on his tried and trusted design partners, the US resort architects Wimberly Allison Tong & Goo, working in collaboration with interior designers Wilson & Associates. They created their great leisure continent in the Bahamas – like their African Lost City – to unusually high standards: the interiors of the rooms, the décor of the restaurant areas, the careful imitation of flora and fauna, all reveal an impressive attention to detail. The only weakness is the collection of art works on display – all of which are dreadful. Not a single name of international repute appears on the long list of commissioned works. But, when it comes down to it, people come here not for a museum of contemporary art – but for fun, fun, fun.

above
Lost and found: Atlantis finally emerges from the seas as a hyper-resort, right on the shore of Paradise Island in the Bahamas.

opposite
Black pearl: below the staircase in the main lobby, a giant shell holds a solid granite pearl, revolving on a jet of water.

next spread
Great Hall of Waters: the domed lobby space of the Royal Towers.

top
Mayan waterslides: the
fun attraction is a
pastiche of the old temple
architecture of the
Mexican Yucatan
peninsula. Those who dare
can glide right into an
underwater glass tube,
which leads safely
through a shark-filled
lagoon.

above
Overlooking Atlantis:
guest room in the Royal
Towers, with private
sundeck.

left
The Dig: the subterranean
labyrinth is an
entertaining walkway
through the treasures of
the sea.

hideaway hotels

The tide is turning. Travel once again represents getting away from day-to-day routines, from a familiar socio-cultural context, through immersion in another culture or in unspoiled natural environments, and the discovery of far-off worlds — but also of new worlds of experience for the spirit and the soul. However, it is one of the contradictions of today's globalized tourist industry that these places of refuge from urban life exert their attraction by offering all the comforts of that very civilization, even in the middle of nowhere. Adventure has become no more than stylish relaxation in an artificial idyll, comfort in the wilderness: this is the price we pay for preserving hidden corners of the natural world, whose survival could scarcely be financed any other way than by the tourist dollar. One of the most important new developments in hotel design is the ethnographic appropriation of local styles, the amalgamation of disparate, imaginative vocabularies drawn from East and West. This trend may look like retrospection, but could in fact be a new pluralism, drawing on many cultural sources and various eras, and having nothing in common with the unsubtle comic-style imitations of the flashy entertainment resorts.

relax in style

Miracle Manor Retreat

Desert Hot Springs, USA 1998	Architecture/Interior design: Michael Rotondi, April Greiman

IN both architecture and pop music, the 1970s was the era of the supergroups. Together with avant-garde teams such as Archigram and Superstudio, from 1971 onwards the Californian outfit Morphosis was part of the experimental architectural vanguard. Like the legendary rock bands, Morphosis had its high-profile departures. Ten years ago the co-founder Michael Rotondi left to pursue a solo career. At that time he can hardly have imagined that he would one day have a second career as a hotel proprietor, but today he is the proud owner of the tiny Miracle Manor Retreat – having transformed an old desert motel near Palm Springs into a minimalist paradise, a six-room hideaway complete with hot baths filled from its own mineral springs.

Rotondi's creative partner in the project was his wife April Greiman, one of the USA's most widely renowned graphic designers. The two of them stumbled on the hotel property by chance. Built in 1948, it consisted of three buildings set around a green inner courtyard. The windows of the guest rooms looked out over the square, offering views of rare botanical displays rather than of the arid expanses of the surrounding desert.

Rotondi and Greiman put their plan into action almost as soon as the purchase was complete. 'The objective was to make a retreat in the desert with an environment totally dedicated to encouraging a contemplative state of mind,' they explain. 'The restoration of the buildings and the rooms was intended to let the desert pass completely through the site, enhancing the experience of landscape, occupied space and architecture. The interior design is less than visible and the architecture is quiet.' The new window openings in the sparsely furnished rooms provide panoramic views reminiscent of murals. Instead of cupboards, there are storage chests on wheels under the beds. There is no internet access at Miracle Manor nor

any telephone link to the outside world. Visitors to this remote oasis come in search of relaxation, solitude and uplifting simplicity.

Desert Hot Springs is in Coachella Valley, two hours' drive from Los Angeles, where in spring the meltwaters from the surrounding mountain ranges collect in underground granite caves. Some of the water is tapped in the form of hot springs, which can reach temperatures of up to 100°C (212°F). At Miracle Manor this water is pumped directly into the pool and the thermal bath. Water for the guest rooms and the kitchens is pumped from cold underground springs.

This isolated holistic motel continues to evolve. New ideas are put into practice as soon as they take shape. Rather than doing experiments on paper or in model form, Michael Rotondi is experimenting with reality itself – which seems to suggest that the restless spirit of the 1970s is alive and kicking in this quiet place amid the desert sands.

In the middle of nowhere: an old desert motel was transformed into a spa retreat.

left
Bath house: the hot, steaming pool extends beyond the glass wall to the outside.

opposite
Minimalist refuge: the wings of the former motel have been kept. Architectural alterations were carefully executed to create a pure, ascetic feeling.

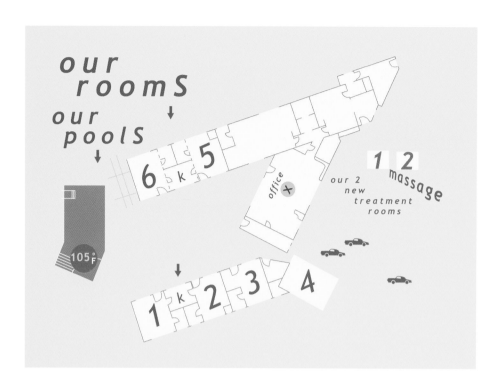

our
roomS
our
pools

6 k 5

105°F

office
X

our 2
new
treatment
rooms

1 2 massage

1 k 2 3 4

above
Site plan.

left
The bare minimum: guest accommodation is deliberately basic. Storage is located under the bed; there are no pictures on the walls, just views of the desert.

right
Where airiness reigns: view from a guest room towards an inner courtyard with pool.

Rajvilas

Jaipur, India 1998	Architecture: Prabhat Pakti Interior design: H. L. Lim & Associates Landscape design: Bill Bensley

FOUNDED in 1934 and still run by the Oberoi family, the Oberoi group is the only one in India to have joined the international luxury hotel élite. With 37 hotels in the five-star category, it is now represented in six other countries, including Indonesia, Mauritius and Egypt. CEO Vikram Oberoi ushered in a new era of exclusive luxury for his company in 1998 when he invented an original concept for small luxury hotels with the Rajvilas in Jaipur: 'I've had my fill of running hotels. It's building them that excites me. I wanted the hotel to capture the princely style of living that Rajasthan is famous for. I said, "Let's build a fort."'

All around in the picturesque Rajasthani capital of Jaipur are historic examples of fabulous accommodation cheek by jowl with powerful fortifications. The city – founded in the early 17th century by the astronomer king Jai Singh II – has mighty walls, splendid gates, and the Maharaja Palace as its magnificent centrepiece. The scientist monarch had observatories built all over India – the largest and best preserved of which, Jantar Mantar, is in Jaipur. In company such as this, it was natural for Oberoi to reach for the stars – and Jaipur ranks high among the subcontinent's luxury tourist destinations. On the eastern outskirts of the city, on 13 hectares (32 acres) of open land – a plot containing only a traditional country house and a 250-year-old Shiva temple – the fantasy architecture of Rajvilas took shape, at a cost of US $20 million, in the form of an inviting fortress surrounded by scattered groups of guest villas. The temple remained as it was, while the

former country house has become a delightful spa and fitness centre.

Immaculate designs for the project were the work of an international team: the Indian architect Prabhat Pakti, the interior design company H. L. Lim & Associates from Singapore, and landscape designer Bill Bensley from the USA. All the architectural forms and ornamentation are derived directly from the traditional stylistic vocabulary of Rajasthan and create an authentic impression without falling into the mannerist trap. The designers have been supremely successful in achieving the high level of comfort expected by the hotel's affluent international clientele without any stylistic inconsistencies. Their concept, as project architect Jeffrey A Wilkes from H. L. Lim & Associates explains, is an entirely convincing one: 'Rajasthani architecture is overpowering, that was a given. We tried to soften the interiors. We wanted the guests to feel like they'd travelled across the desert and stumbled upon the perfect shelter. All of that softness – the draped canopy and abundance of fabrics – is meant to contrast with the hardness of the landscape. The room is cosy and secure, but we used trunks and roll-up mats and folding chairs to create the illusion that it's movable.'

A total of 71 guest rooms are arranged around the battlemented main building, which houses the reception and restaurant. A particular attraction, alongside the three large villas with their own pools, are the hotel's 14 unusual tent constructions, adding a nomadic style of romanticism.

left
Brand-new Rajasthani architecture: the hotel complex is a perfect replica of an old fort.

opposite
A real dreamscape: pavilions, fountains and pool, which at night are illuminated.

Stairway to heaven: grand
steps create a multi-level
playground for guests.

top and above
Luxury home for nomads: guest villas have tent-roofed bedrooms and bathrooms that feature free-standing tubs and which open onto private courtyards.

above right
Immaculate reproduction: the ornamentation and form of the lobby hall follow the style of classic feudal Rajasthan buildings.

Pousada Santa Maria do Bouro

Bouro, Portugal 1997	Architecture/Interior design: Eduardo Souto de Moura

NOT far from Braga in northern Portugal, in the small village of Boura, is a former Cistercian monastery founded in 1162. After a long period of decline, all that survived of the establishment was a decaying 18th-century structure. An architect commissioned to restore the building and convert it into a top-class country hotel would find it hard to know where to start.

Eduardo Souto de Moura, the architect asked to undertake the project, explains his approach: 'Between restoration with the aim of preserving the work of architecture and Le Corbusier's philosophy of inserting new materials, forms and functions in existing buildings, I chose the latter. Historic buildings were always forced to change with the times, to adapt themselves to new functions, and they were changed and altered without provoking any moral objections. What fascinates us about a historic city quarter is the various layers associated with different epochs.'

However, the restoration by Souto de Moura – who has worked closely in the past with Alvaro Sizas – will disappoint anyone expecting a radical contrast between the old and new parts of the building. While the new elements are clearly indicated, the historic elements are treated with great respect. In this way, the interventions and additions emphasize the traditional character of the abbey. New brickwork incorporates rubble from the original building and local granite; the brass frames of the re-arranged windows remain invisible from outside; the collapsed gables were replaced with flat roofs covered with vegetation, looking like the natural patina of historic places.

Inside, Souto de Moura has created an ascetic harmony between the new additions and the surviving historical fabric. The best example of this can be seen in the elegantly proportioned steel girders that now hold up the ceilings, in place of the old wooden beams which collapsed long ago. The architect demonstrated a small stroke of genius in the dining room, the former monastery kitchen, where what was once the huge open fireplace has been transformed into a pyramid-shaped skylight. The 33 guest rooms may at

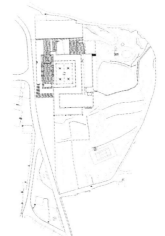

above
Merging of past and present: newly fitted roofs and windows respect the order and character of the historic monastery.

left
Site plan of the Pousada Santa Maria do Bouro complex.

opposite
Austere grace: lobby of the hotel. The new ceilings, with bare iron beams, fit well with the mighty stonework.

first sight resemble monastic cells, but in fact they offer every conceivable five-star facility, including well-concealed air conditioning. They are arranged around two internal courtyards, one of which is the reconstructed cloister, the other a small, U-shaped orange grove.

The hotel, which opened in 1997, is the 22nd regeneration project undertaken by the state-owned Enatur-Pousadas de Portugal. For nearly 60 years the company has worked to develop high-quality amenities for tourists all over Portugal, while at the same time conserving the country's architectural heritage, including castles, stately homes and monasteries. They are not under pressure to show short-term profitability – their priority is to preserve historic buildings through sensitive conversions – and so guests have the privilege, as at Santa Maria do Bouro, of enjoying impressive historic architecture whose impact has not been watered down by the need for compromise.

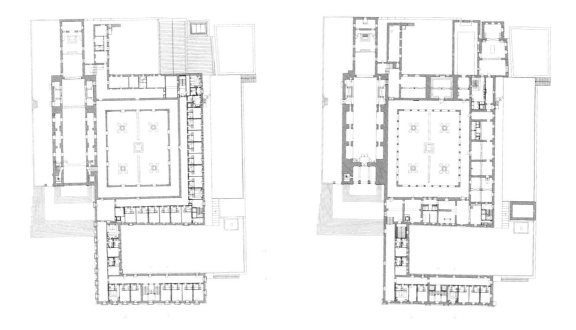

top left and right
Plans of the second (left) and first floors.

above
What the monks were missing: pool area down the hill in the former monastery garden.

Five-star cloister cell: the interiors of the guest rooms feature minimalist design with high-quality detailing.

Ngorongoro Crater Lodge

Ngorongoro, Tanzania 1997	Architecture: Silvio Rech Interior design: Chris Browne

THE Ngorongoro crater is unquestionably one of the most beautiful places in Africa to experience the illusion of a natural and animal kingdom untouched by humans. The forest-covered edge of the 20 kilometre (12¹/₂ mile) wide crater, set at an altitude of 2,359 metres (7,740 feet), offers a view over the savannah 600 metres (1,970 feet) below, where elephants and herds of antelopes range through the hazy grasslands. This sublime landscape, neighbouring the Serengeti national park, has long been on Unesco's list of World Heritage sites, so it was for good reason that Conservation Corporation Africa (CCA), which operates top-quality game lodges in South Africa, Namibia, Kenya and Zanzibar, invested in this particular spot of Tanzania. The Ngorongoro Crater Lodge occupies the site of a row of corrugated-metal bungalows, privately built for hunting purposes in 1934, which had been converted into a plain, functional bush hotel after Tanzania became independent in 1961.

The architect entrusted with the project was Silvio Rech, a South African who had already designed the Makalali private game reserve in Transvaal (which opened the year before) for the CCA. As with the earlier project, Rech lived on the site with his family throughout the construction period so that he could work alongside the local craftsmen implementing his designs: 'The brief was for an unobtrusive, low-key exterior and an interior that looked as if some travelling colonial like Lord Delamere had unpacked his trunks of favourite silver-ware and other treasures from home, along with whatever he'd collected on his travels through Africa.' Together with his partner Chris Browne, who was responsible for the interior design, Silvio Rech created a fantasy world that combined romantic re-creations with delightful stylistic contrasts.

The loosely connected structure of various organic architectural forms, with roofs made of dried banana leaves, has the air of a Masai clay citadel that has survived

intact through the ages, but inside, under the asymmetric domed ceilings, there are glittering chandeliers, magnificent red-and-gold brocade cushions, dainty Empire writing desks, loosely covered chairs, beds with silk coverings, ornate mirrors, luxurious Persian carpets and lavish baths. But the real luxury here is the panoramic view – a view that guests in the 30 suites (each consisting of two round huts) can enjoy not only from their private balconies but also from their bedrooms and baths.

The crater is effectively a unique 'retirement home' for ageing bull elephants, who come here for their last majestic wanderings. There are even about two dozen black rhinos – almost extinct elsewhere – trotting through the bush. Visitors can experience another astonishing drama, played out between lions and hyenas. Packs of hyenas are the most industrious hunters, yet, more often that not, scarcely have they bagged their prey than a group of lions arrives and whips their meal away – one reason why the local big-cat population is higher than anywhere else on the African continent.

above
Village for the tourist tribe: the Ngorongoro Crater Lodge is situated on the top rim of an extinct volcano.

opposite
Colonial romanticism: the interiors of the guest rooms freely mix African elements with remnants of old Europe.

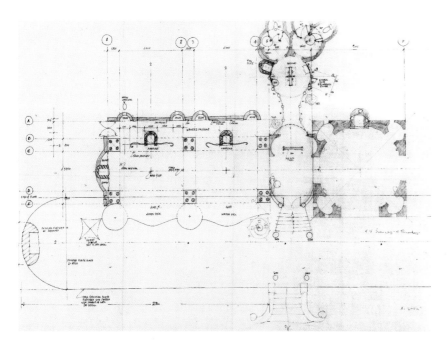

above left
**Site plan of the
Ngorongoro Crater Lodge
complex.**

above
**Retreat from the wildlife:
large fireplace in the lobby
building.**

left
**Gamespotter's tub: the
bathrooms, as well as
bedrooms and living
rooms, offer spectacular
views of the crater plain.**

opposite
**Safari king-sized bedroom
of a guest villa, with
banana-leaf ceiling and
fantasy Masai-style four-
poster playground.**

THE fate of Ischgl in Austria perfectly illustrates how the simple pleasures of Alpine tourism have recently become part of a world of high-octane, fun-filled entertainment. This mountain village in the south-western Tyrol, set at an altitude of 1,376 metres (4,510 feet), once prided itself on having 600 cows. It is now large enough to accommodate 10,000 tourists and is enjoying a new-found affluence. Single travellers can visit the chat room on Ischgl's website to search discreetly for forthcoming holiday affairs, and at night the innumerable discotheques are every bit as busy as the pistes of the Silvretta are during the day. Rock concerts featuring crowd-pulling stars such as Jon Bon Jovi, Tina Turner and Elton John are also held at Ischgl. The Aloys family, well-established hoteliers and restaurateurs, made the shrewd decision to create an oasis of peace and serenity amid all the hustle and bustle of Ischgl by converting the traditional Madlein hotel (which had previously been extended in various stages) into a health spa.

Working in collaboration with the architectural psychologist Hans-Georg Rupp, the Aachen-based firm Mescherowsky Architekten used the opportunity presented by the hotel project to develop an alternative world that focuses on perception, the senses and sensations, and provides physical and aesthetic stimulation for the guests through leisure and relaxation. 'The design concept is straightforward and strict,' explains Sabine Mescherowsky. 'The building and interiors are characterized by simplicity and clear forms. A tightrope walk between extremes: light–dark, smooth–rough, hot–cold, high–deep, narrow–wide. The design as a whole is determined by four basic elements: light, water, fire and air. The use of materials is minimalist, high-quality, simple in its details. Stone, wood and glass.'

The conversion and extension project increased the hotel's gross usable floor space to 5,429 square metres (58,420 square feet) most of which is occupied by the new leisure facilities. At ground level, which has panoramic views of the Alpine scenery, the architects created a swimming pool, sauna, fitness room and a glass-bordered relaxation area with a sunken open fireplace at its centre – all designed in a style inspired by Japanese minimalism. The teak-laid corridor extends beyond the building, becoming a footpath to a hot-spring grotto. In the basement, below the health and fitness area, is a beauty centre. A new glazed staircase connects the guest-room floors of the original building with the suites in the newly added wing. The rooms in the new wing follow the same design principles: extensive glazed areas have the effect of transforming the natural Alpine scenery into a living fresco. Large windows in the bathrooms mean that guests can even enjoy a bath with a view. Those in search of old-fashioned cosiness and less transparency can book the more flowery, Laura Ashley-style rooms in the hotel's old wing.

left
Body zone: the new annexe of the revamped Hotel Madlein is home to a spacious spa and fitness centre.

opposite
Square of fire: the relaxation area, with the sunken open fireplace.

above and left
Minimalism goes Alpine: lounge on one of the guest-room floors and typical guest-room interior in the new hotel wing.

opposite
Temple of health: the pool area is located at the heart of the spa centre.

DEVI GARH was a fortified palace set on one of the three passes leading into the Udaipur valley, which had served as a bastion against Mughal attacks on the Mewar kingdom since 1760. The rock fortress retained its military function until the 1960s, when the region became part of the Indian state of Rajasthan. With its collection of buildings and courtyards arranged over various levels, the majestic complex covers an area of 7,500 square metres (80,700 square feet) and measures 43 metres (141 feet) from its lowest point to its highest. The region's former capital, Udaipur, and its airport lie less than 30 km (19 miles) away. Given that Udaipur is now the second major point of departure after Jaipur for tours of Rajasthan, it was decided to give the palace a new lease of life by converting it into a hotel.

The planning and construction work on Devi Garh lasted three years, and the hotel finally opened in late 1999, in time for the millennium celebrations. Rajiv Saini, the architect responsible for the renovation project (which cost 160 million rupees), achieved his aim convincingly. 'It took me a while to synthesize an approach that was minimal and contemporary and that would at the same time sit in harmony with the 240-year-old fortified palace,' he admits. 'It involved a series of interventions throughout the palace using modern building materials to forge an uninterrupted link that symbolizes the desire for intimacy between the old and the new. The emphasis was on innovating with local craft traditions and skills to create an environment that would be refreshing yet restful for the guests.'

The old building has been converted with great care. The 23 luxury suites are arranged in groups over the various levels of the palace complex, each overlooking an internal courtyard. Installing a single central lift shaft would have distorted the historical ground plan, so three separate lifts were built instead and connected by walkways to take visitors from reception up to the top storey. Installation of air conditioning and sanitation systems was complicated because the architect wanted to avoid as far as possible

having to break through the huge load-bearing stone walls. The solution was to raise the floor levels; where the existing structure had suitable niches and bays, these were used to house the necessary pipework and controls. Fixtures and fittings, including the furnishings, avoid historical reminiscence in terms of form, although they do use regionally or culturally appropriate materials and techniques. The guest suites, lobby areas and restaurant facilities are all ascetic in style; even the abundance of semi-precious stones used for decorative purposes does little to alter the prevailing air of unadorned simplicity. As a result, the conversion is a triumph of harmony that neither conceals nor distorts the spirit of the place.

From the Durbar Hall lobby, the conference lounge, restaurant, bar, billiards room and library through to the arts and recreation hall, tennis room, gymnasium and health club, Devi Garh represents a brilliantly recreated expedition into the past. Guests who want to take a closer look at the wild mountain passes in the surrounding area can do so – by camel rather than four-wheel-drive vehicle, if they are feeling particularly adventurous.

opposite
Pool in the yard: a former court was converted into a plunge area.

below
Fortress guarding Rajasthan: the military outpost built in 1760 now offers 23 luxury suites.

above
Durbar Hall lobby: as in
many other parts of
the historic monumental
building, the original
materials were restored to
their former splendour.

opposite
Relaxing stronghold:
main pool deck,
surrounded by the tops
of the fortification walls.

Palau Sa Font

Palma de Mallorca, Spain, 2000	Architecture: Andreu Benassar Interior design: Hans-Jürgen Pahl

MALLORCA has been through several incarnations as a tourist retreat. From the early 19th century onwards the Mediterranean island was a romantic hotspot for aristocratic and educated travellers; in the 20th century it became first a favourite place in the sun for wealthy English tourists, then a prime destination for millions of package-holiday travellers, and finally an irresistible magnet for German property investors. The latest invasion is no longer restricted to coastal areas and idyllic regions – it has long since embraced the island's capital, Palma, whose old town is undergoing a rapid gentrification as a result of the new influx of capital.

It was no coincidence, therefore, that the new four-star Palau Sa Font hotel was located in Palma, set in a palace built more than three centuries earlier, in which the bishop himself is supposed once to have lived. Most recently, the building was used as an art gallery. When hotel operator Tom Gösmann, who had emigrated to Mallorca from Cologne, started on this project on the Calle Apuntadores four years ago, little stood in the way of a dynamic conversion. Only the façade, with its Moorish windows, was legally protected. The Mallorcan architect Andreu Benassar was free to reorganize the interior of the building as he wished.

What makes the little Palau Sa Font stand out in the relatively unexciting world of the Balearic hotel industry is the thoroughly modern interior design by Berlin-based designer Hans-Jürgen Pahl. Instead of misguidedly aping local traditions in the search for the 'true' Mallorca, Pahl sought to achieve a distinctive, original contemporary style using traditional techniques and materials. 'We have tried to combine opposites in a harmonious whole,' he explains. A traditional decorative cement technique in a contemporary pattern was used for the floors. Most of the furniture was specially designed and produced in Manacor, a Mallorcan town specializing in furniture production. For the table frames, beds and light fittings, Pahl used rustic wrought-iron with an artificial patina. Four dominant colours – red, yellow, orange and light green – run through the entire building, from the ground floor with its reception, breakfast room and broken-tiled bar, via the pool patio on the first storey and the guest floors, through to the belvedere, or lookout tower, on the roof.

The conversion created space for 19 rooms and suites – including the former chapel – and a conference room. Many of the guests are professionals who stay at Palau Sa Font for a few days of relaxation combined with intensive brainstorming or planning. After work they can relax in the jacuzzi, surrounded by the Moorish old city walls, or sit with a glass of wine in the semi-open lookout tower, enjoying an impressive, panoramic vista of the city at sunset – with a clear view of the cathedral towers, the harbour and the sea.

left
In the shade of Palma's cathedral: rooftop of Palau Sa Font, with small pool area.

Behind old walls: the Moorish windows are the only sign of the past. The interiors of the guest rooms were designed in a restrained, contemporary way.

above
Bright colours: the corridor to the guest rooms shows how the four leading tones — red, yellow, orange and light green — run through the entire hotel.

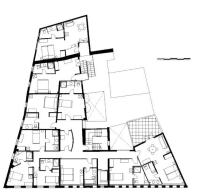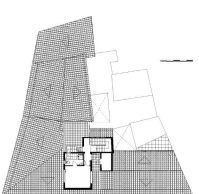

above
Away from the street life: ground-floor bar of the hotel.

left
Floor plans.

Explora en Atacama

San Pedro, Chile 1998	Architecture/Interior design: German del Sol

SAN Pedro has long been an oasis. It was probably 3,000 years ago that South American Indians founded the first settlement on the eastern edge of the Atacama desert, marking the furthest point of penetration by the meltwaters of the Andes. And it was the Spaniard Francisco de Aguirre – the notorious conquistador whose Amazonian exploits were immortalized by film-maker Werner Herzog – who inflicted defeat on the nearby Indian fortress of Quitero in 1540, with thirty armoured horsemen. What followed – the boom era of the saltpetre mines in the 19th century and the exploitation up to the present day of vast copper deposits – largely bypassed the little town of San Pedro set at an altitude of more than 2,500 metres (8,200 feet).

San Pedro remained a sleepy place until a few years ago, when it became a favourite haunt of drop-outs fleeing contemporary civilization – after which some of the more adventurous independent tourists began to find their way there, too. Its remote location and the archaeological museum established there by the former Jesuit priest Gustave Le Paige are not the only attractions of the town. San Pedro is also ideally located for the Tatio geysers, the flamingo colonies of the huge salt lake called Salar de Atacama and the bizarre Moon Valley. So it is no coincidence that the second Explora hotel designed by the Chilean architect German del Sol was built in San Pedro; his first project was in the far south of Chile, on Lago Puyehue in the Torres del Paine national park, in the cold of Patagonia.

The fact that the Explora is located away from the centre of San Pedro offers clues to its exotic character. Del Sol avoids unimaginative borrowings from traditional local styles. The white, telescoped volumes of the irregular lozenge-shaped ground plan, surmounted by irregular copper-covered roofs, may seem the epitome of modernism, but they also have contextual relevance.

'Architecture in Atacama is challenged to get strength out of weakness, and joy out of the essentials...to relate the hotel with the culture of the place, the trembling beauty of its arts and crafts...like wrinkles in an interesting face,' says del Sol. 'Architecture may capture the grace of ruins that everyone interprets at will, the vagueness of broken line walls that enclose the space gently, because their forms are determined by real needs of life, not by abstract certainities.'

Around the main building, which houses the hotel's restaurant, bar and lounge, are the lower guest wings, with 52 rooms. This capacity will soon double on completion of a second phase of construction. Del Sol also designed the stables near the hotel. This desert hideaway cost about US $15 million – and must attract an affluent clientele in order to repay such an investment. Some of the ageing hippies who have settled in San Pedro fear an invasion by the jet set. The occasional member of Europe's glittering aristocracy has already been spotted in the Explora. But, if San Pedro managed to survive Aguirre, it will surely be able to cope with Camilla Parker-Bowles & Co.

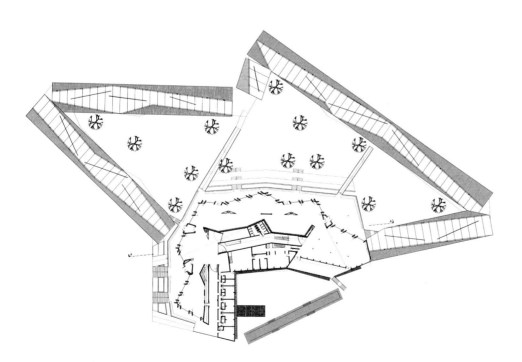

top
Water in the driest place on earth: pool pavilion of the Explora en Atacama resort.

left
Site plan of the hotel complex, showing the sculptured roofscape of the different wings.

right
Deconstructed forms: skylight and fireplace form irregular shapes, which are a dominant feature of Explora en Atacama's architecture.

Anassa Hotel

Polis, Cyprus 1998	Architecture: Sandy & Babcock Associates Interior design: James Northcutt Associates; Darrell Schmitt Design Associates

FOR decades, Cyprus has been politically divided and regarded by some as a downmarket destination for sun-worshipping package tourists, and its reputation has suffered unjustly. According to ancient Greek myth, the island was the home of Aphrodite, goddess of beauty – legend has it that she bathed under a small waterfall near the Akamas peninsula in the north-west of the island. This area, which included the ancient Greek capital of Marion, was once the island's political centre.

Today the site is occupied by the town of Polis, which since 1998 has been home to a new resident – another undisputed beauty – bearing the ancient Greek name of Anassa, meaning 'queen'. This was the name chosen by the Cypriot hotel group Thanos for its most ambitious project to date: a five-star complex that blends in harmoniously with the undulating rocky slopes of Chrysochou Bay. Individual one- to three-storey guest villas are loosely grouped around a splendid central residence.

Surrounded by lush vegetation, and lavishly equipped with spa and bathing facilities, the Anassa sets the highest standards – standards that are rarely equalled even on more developed Mediterranean islands. According to the Californian architects Sandy & Babcock Associates, 'The complex has been designed as a series of buildings stepping down the hillside, in the manner of a traditional Mediterranean hill town. Maintaining a design sympathetic to its Greek Cypriot surroundings and creating an air of sophisticated luxury were the two primary goals for this unique resort.' The interior design, also the work of Californians, combines traditional elements and motifs with the modern fashion for restraint and clarity of effect.

The Anassa covers 18,580 square metres (199,900 square feet) in total and has more than 184 rooms, around half of them in detached villas and half in the main building. The latter houses three of the four restaurants plus the bar and the entrance to the 'village square' – which even has a small church for couples who come here to get married. A professional conference facility was also included in the hope that the Anassa would become a prime destination for upmarket business events.

The hotel's location in north-west Cyprus, which is less popular with tourists than other parts of the island, is a distinct advantage, especially now that nearby Paphos is served by regular international flights, which means that hotel guests from abroad no longer have to put up with a car journey from Larnaka airport lasting two and a half hours.

opposite
Grand entrance: staircase in the main building of the Anassa Hotel.

left
Stretching down the hillside: the hotel complex is constructed on different levels along the coast.

left
**High ceilings: guest rooms
feature four-poster beds
in double-height spaces.**

right
**Mediterranean heaven:
sundeck with splash pool.**

below
**Site plan of the Anassa
Hotel complex.**

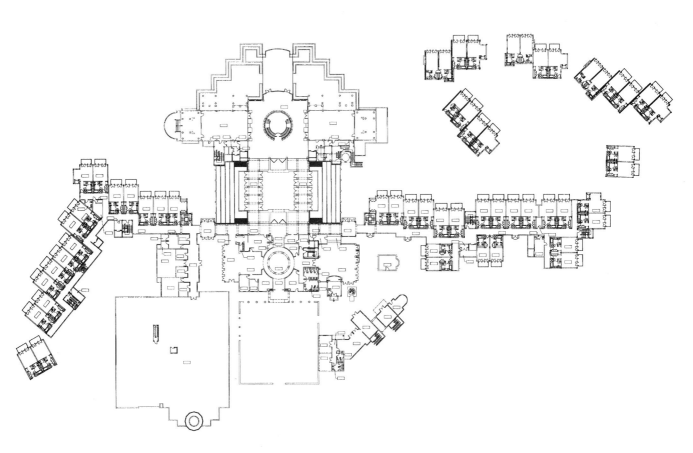

Four Seasons Resort at Sayan

| Bali, Indonesia, 1998 | Architecture/Interior design: Heah & Company |

DESPITE a great deal of initial opposition from local people, in early 1998 the smallest and most exclusive project to date by the luxury Four Seasons hotel chain was completed not far from the town of Ubud, a centre for the arts, in the mountainous inland region of Bali. Unlike many other tourist projects on the island, this hotel was not a simple imitation of Balinese style. Instead, the architect John Heah, originally from Malaysia but then working in London, had been brave enough to experiment with relatively audacious modern architecture. The fact that the building was also (and quite visibly) constructed mainly in concrete aroused further indignation.

The agitation generated at the time is hard to comprehend now. The Resort at Sayan, nestling on terraced slopes above the Ayung river, is utterly imbued with respect for the character of its beautiful surroundings. 'When I saw the site, I decided to build the hotel along the side of the ridge rather than putting it on top. I wanted it to melt into the landscape,' says Heah, who believes that the finished building fulfils his intention in every respect. The inspiration behind the architectural design was the idea of flowing, diving, descending from the top of the mountain down into the valley. Guests arrive at the top of the site, on the crest of the hill, and cross a 60 metre (197 foot) long bridge spanning a deep ravine to reach a pavilion, set in the middle of a circular lotus pond (covering an impressive 850 square metres (9,145 square feet)). The pavilion turns out to be the roof of the main building, with stairs down to the reception, lobby and Jati bar. Down another staircase is

the Ayung Terrace restaurant, and on the very lowest level is the luxuriously equipped health and fitness area.

Two curved side wings with a total of 18 rooms and suites flank the central elliptical structure. It is more expensive to stay in the 28 guest villas which, surrounded by delicately splashing water terraces, are dotted about on the hillside leading down to the river. The villas are constructed on the same pattern as the main building, with an entrance at the top level and a winding staircase leading down to the bedrooms and living rooms, all rounded off with outdoor terraces and a private plunge pool. The main swimming pool and the hotel's second restaurant, the Riverside Pool café, are located on the riverbank. Guests who prefer to be closer to nature can take a dip in the cool waters of the Ayung.

Construction costs of around US $30 million for this extraordinary hotel seem astonishingly modest. Yet Heah combined local craftsmanship and contemporary building techniques in just as skilful a way as he had adapted his architectural plans to the topographical conditions. To avoid using heavy construction machinery on this rough terrain, the buildings were cast in small sections in local concrete, and all the wood and metal work was carried out by local workers – which helped to reconcile the local people to a project that had been so unpopular to start with. On an island that has not escaped the destructive effects of international tourism, the Four Seasons Resort has won many awards and is held up as a model of contemporary, low-impact luxury accommodation.

left
Section of the hotel site, showing the entrance bridge over the ravine to the main building.

above
**Closer to nature: pond in one
of the guest villas, which
are scattered on a hillside,
along the Ayung river.**

Cascading corridor: rock walls, with falling water, and streams line the walkways to the guest rooms in the central building.

above
Luxury of seclusion:
ground floor of a guest
villa, with private sundeck
and pool.

right
Panoramic dining: Ayung
Terrace restaurant in
the main hotel building.

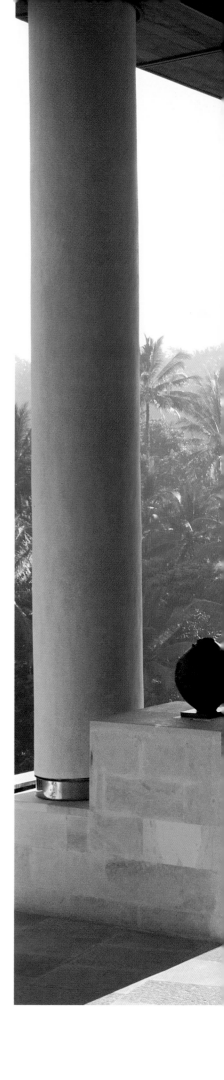

Casa Teygoyo

| Conil, Lanzarote 1999 | Architecture/Interior design: Heidi Hupe |

A LANDSCAPE of strong contrasts, alternating abruptly between rough wilderness and areas of placid calmness, and including black volcanic fields, red mountain ridges and hidden botanical treasures, characterizes Lanzarote, the most north-easterly of the Canary Islands. When, in 1994, Unesco declared the whole of Lanzarote a reserve for science, education and the arts, it confirmed the special status of the island, which had remained relatively untroubled by the less appealing aspects of mass tourism. A key figure in this respect was the artist–architect Cesar Manrique, who, until his accidental death in 1992, did everything he could to preserve Lanzarote's traditions and individuality – and not only through the many exemplary buildings he himself designed. The restrictive planning regulations Manrique forced through ensured that any tourist development on the island was governed by ecological and cultural considerations at an early stage.

Its harmonious balance between preservation and progress attracted many visitors to Lanzarote. Some stayed, including the German interior designer Heidi Hupe. A few years ago she acquired a country house in the region of La Geria, between the Montañas Chupaderos and Guardilama, where Malvasia vines grow in funnel-shaped hollows bordered by semicircular-shaped walls made of loosely piled lava stones. Traditionally, the island's wealthy families would retire up here in summer to escape the burning winds blowing through the island's capital Arrecife.

The oldest parts of Heidi Hupe's country house, now the Casa Teygoyo hotel, date from the 18th century. 'Of course the aim of the conversion,' she explains, 'was to create a small hotel with all the necessary amenities, without damaging the valuable fabric of the existing building.' Drawing on her previous experience as a successful restaurant owner, she tackled the business of creating a hotel with a high degree of professionalism. On a usable floor space of 1,000 square metres (10,760 square feet) she incorporated 12 rooms, a restaurant, a bar and a conference room; a pool area in two sections, including a 22 metre (72 foot) swimming pool, was created in the 5,000 square metre (53,800 square foot) gardens.

All Casa Teygoyo's interiors are in the island's traditional colours of ochre, indigo and pillar-box red. Except for a few local antiques, the furnishings are functional and sensitively chosen: metal four-poster beds, simple wooden furniture, white loose covers. The bathrooms are decorated with local mosaic tiles; some of them have built-in showers, others have freestanding baths. The traditional advantage of the location – the mild summer climate – also benefits this country hotel, which opened in late 1999. Here, away from the buzz on the coast, Lanzarote can be enjoyed all year round. For beach-lovers the sea is within reach.

left
Oasis in black lava: Casa Teygoyo, with guest apartments facing the pool deck.

opposite
Inner calm: the old country house's courtyard forms the heart of the small hotel.

left
Matching the past: the bathrooms show an appreciation of traditional Lanzarote colours and tiles.

right
Teygoyo suite: the guest rooms feature upholstery with white loose covers and functional metal furniture.

Icehotel

Jukkasjärvi, Sweden 2001	Architecture/Interior design: Arne Bergh and Ake Larsson

IT all started with an arts event. In the depths of winter 1989, in the Lapland village of Jukkasjärvi, in the far north of Sweden, a few enterprising people used ice to build a pavilion-style gallery on the thick ice-sheet covering the Torne river. Many people who came to see the ice gallery reacted as if it were an igloo and expressed a desire to spend the night in it – and this is how the idea for the Icehotel was born. Since then, the building of an Icehotel – which survives only as long as the Arctic temperatures remain low enough – has become an annual event, and the structures have become bigger and bolder every year: the 2001 version covered a surface area of no less than 5,000 square metres (53,800 square feet).

Work on building the Icehotel begins each November. The larger arches are made of a mixture of snow and ice, while pillars and internal fittings are made of pure river ice. As the new year starts, the hotel is officially opened and guests begin to arrive. In 2001 the hotel achieved a new record, taking more than 9,000 bookings for its icy double rooms (where the temperature is between -4° and -9°C (29° and 16°F)). By late April, as spring approaches, the end is near. The entire building – including the bar, the chapel and the cinema – simply melts away.

Swedish artists Arne Bergh and Ake Larsson have been responsible for the design and creation of each version of the Icehotel. Working in collaboration with numerous other sculptors, they shape the basic structure (which hardens over metal frames that are later removed) and create all the architectural details such as pillars, windows and doors, as well as fittings and furnishings – bar counters, tables, chairs, benches, beds, lights and sculptures. All the materials are supplied by the River Torne. Even the drinks, such as the infamous Wolfspaw, are served in tumblers made of ice. 'Every night is different,' says Arne Bergh. 'Sometimes it can be quiet and still, other nights people are singing and dancing, and sometimes the whole place goes crazy – I won't say which nationalities are present those nights.' Guests sit on reindeer skins and sleep in arctic sleeping bags, and for those who feel uneasy about sleeping in the ice there are simple, conventionally heated wooden huts next door.

The hotel's continuing success has created an appetite for more in Jukkasjärvi. Ice is now used to draw the crowds throughout the year, regardless of the weather. May 2000 saw the opening, in a large refrigerated hall, of the Icehotel Art Centre, which presents ice sculptures and relics preserved from the thawed hotel; the latest attraction is a group of indoor igloos, which guests can crawl into for the night, even in summer. Some of the frozen treasures of Lapland – handmade tumblers, sculptures, even entire bar counters made of ice – are now made to order and exported as far as Asia.

opposite
Crystal palace: vaulted lounge, with translucent furniture and chandelier, all made out of river ice.

left
Lapland's pride: entrance to the Icehotel, which is rebuilt every Arctic winter.

next spread
Below zero: in the guest room, reindeer skins serve as warming covers.

above
Deep freeze: guests who dare spend the night in polar-proof sleeping bags (top left); the Auratic Chapel was a new addition in the 2001 Icehotel (top right); in the bar, the giant vodka bottle honours one of the main sponsors (above left); even tumblers and other accessories are made from ice (above right).

opposite
Monumental hallway: the only reinforcements inside the ice structure are invisible steel frames.

project information

NAME: THE HOTEL
ADDRESS: Sempacherstrasse 14
CH-6002 Luzern
Tel: + 41 41 226 86 86
Fax: + 41 41 226 86 90
E-mail: info@the-hotel.ch
Web: www.the-hotel.ch
ROOMS/FACILITIES: 25 rooms (10 Splendid Garden and Park
Deluxe Suites (with patio garden), 5 Corner
Junior Suites, 10 Deluxe Studios); 'Bam Bou'
restaurant; 'The Lounge' bar
COMPLETION: 2000
CLIENT: Urs Karli
OPERATOR: Urs Karli
ARCHITECTURE & DESIGN: Architectures Jean Nouvel
SUBCONTRACTORS/SUPPLIERS: Daniel Laurent (project manager); Rebsamen
Elektroplanung (electricity); Partner Plan AG
(ventilation); Kramit Sanitar AG (sanitation);
Emmer Pfenniger Partner AG (façade);
Martinelli & Menti AG (heating); Alain Bony
(colour concept); Romano Bassi (graphics)

NAME: SANDERSON
ADDRESS: 50 Berners Street
London W1P 4AD
Tel: + 44 (0)20 7300 1400
Fax: + 44 (0)20 7300 1401
ROOMS/FACILITIES: 150 rooms; 2 deluxe penthouse apartments;
gym; billiards room; gourmet speciality shop
with takeout service; international news,
magazine and gift shop; full-service business
centre; multi-service meeting spaces and
hospitality suites; executive boardroom;
private conference facility; courtyard garden;
'Agua Bathhouse'; 'Spoon+' restaurant; 'Long
Bar'; 'Purple Bar'
COMPLETION: 2000
CLIENT: Ian Schrager
OPERATOR: I.S.U.K. Management Ltd.
ARCHITECTURE & DESIGN: Philippe Starck
SUBCONTRACTORS/SUPPLIERS: Rita Schrager, Leila Fazel ('Agua Bathhouse');
Fabien Baron, Lisa Atkin, Melissa Sison (art
direction); Michael Nash Associates (graphic
design/room amenities); Jean Baptiste
Mondino, Ninety Nine (video installations);
Isometrix, Arnold Chan (lighting); Madison Cox,
Marie Christine de Laubarede (landscape
consultant)

NAME: SIDE HOTEL
ADDRESS: Drehbahn 49

D-20354 Hamburg
Tel: + 49 (0)40 30 99 90
Fax: + 49 (0)40 30 99 93 99
E-mail: SIDE-hotel@gmx.de
Web: www.seaside-hotels.de
ROOMS/FACILITIES: 178 rooms and suites, including 10 'flying'
suites; 6 conference rooms; private lounges;
ballroom; 'fusion' restaurant; bar; 'SPA' with
pool; gym; sauna
COMPLETION: 2001
CLIENT: Seaside Hotels
OPERATOR: Seaside Hotels
ARCHITECTURE: Alsop & Störmer Architekten
INTERIOR DESIGN: Matteo Thun
SUBCONTRACTORS: Robert Wilson (light choreographer)

NAME: ST MARTIN'S LANE
ADDRESS: 45 St. Martin's Lane
London WC2N 4HX
Tel: + 44 (0)20 7300 5500
Fax: + 44 (0)20 7300 5501
ROOMS/FACILITIES: 204 rooms; two deluxe penthouse
apartments; gymnasium; Multimedia
Entertainment Theatre; 'The Light Bar'; 'Asia de
Cuba' restaurant; 'The Sea Bar'; 'Saint M'
brasserie; 'The Sidewalk Café' and outdoor
garden restaurant; 'Rum Bar'; Lumière
Cinéma; multi-service meeting spaces and
hospitality suites; private conference facility
COMPLETION: 1999
CLIENT: Ian Schrager
OPERATOR: I.S.U.K Management Ltd.
ARCHITECTUR & DESIGN: Philippe Starck
SUBCONTRACTORS/SUPPLIERS: Fabien Baron, Lisa Atkin, Melissa Sison (art
direction); Michael Nash Associates (graphic
design/room amenities); Jean Baptiste
Mondino (video installations); Arnold Chan
(lighting); Madison Cox (landscape
consultant)

NAME: HOTEL GREIF
ADDRESS: Piazza Walther
Waltherplatz
1-39100 Bolzano
Bozen
Tel: (0)471 318 000
Fax: (0)471 318 148
E-mail: info@greif.it
Web: www.greif.it
ROOMS/FACILITIES: 33 rooms; restaurant; 'Laurin' bar; pool;
meeting and banquet rooms available at

neighbouring Parkhotel Laurin

COMPLETION: 2000
CLIENT: Franz Staffler
OPERATOR: Franz Staffler
ARCHITECTURE: Boris Podrecca
INTERIOR DESIGN: Rooms individually designed by local artists
SUBCONTRACTORS: Bartenbach of Innsbruck (lighting)

NAME: THE STANDARD
ADDRESS: 8300 Sunset Blvd
West Hollywood CA 90069
Tel: + 1 323 650 9090
ROOMS/FACILITIES: 140 rooms; pool; lounge; bar; barber shop;
tattoo parlour; 24-hour restaurant; nightclub
COMPLETION: 1999
CLIENT: André Balazs
OPERATOR: André Balazs
ARCHITECTURE: Adam Tihany
INTERIOR DESIGN: Shawn Hausman
SUBCONTRACTORS/SUPPLIERS: Martha Schwarz (landscape architect)

NAME: THE HUDSON
ADDRESS: 356 West 58 Street
New York NY 10019
Tel: + 1 (212) 554 6000
Fax: + 1 (212) 554 6001
E-mail: info@hudson.schragerhotels.com
Web: www.hudsonhotel.com
ROOMS/FACILITIES: 1,000 rooms; exhibition kitchen restaurant;
lobby bar; 'Library Bar'; private park;
conference facilities; business centre;
boutiques/shops
COMPLETION: 2000
CLIENT: Ian Schrager
OPERATOR: Ian Schrager Management
ARCHITECTURE & INTERIOR DESIGN: Philippe Starck

NAME: MOJIKO HOTEL
ADDRESS: 9-11 Minato-Machi
Moji-Ku, Kitakyushu-shi
Fukuoka 801-0852
Japan
Tel: 011 81 93 321 1111
ROOMS/FACILITIES: 134 rooms, including 4 suites and 3 Japanese
suites; 'Spazio' event hall; 'Gioia' banquet hall;
'Eterno' ceremony hall; 'Portone' trattoria; 'Bar
Tempo'; 'Ichiju-An' Japanese tea room
COMPLETION: 2000
CLIENT: Kita-Kyushu City, Mojiko Development
Corporation

OPERATOR: K.K. Mojiko Hotel
ARCHITECTURE: Aldo Rossi
INTERIOR DESIGN: Shigeru Uchida
SUBCONTRACTORS/SUPPLIERS: Matsushita Electric Works Ltd., Daiko
(lighting); Cast, ILU, ums Pastoe bv (furniture)

NAME: ATOLL HOTEL
ADDRESS: Lung Wai 27
27498 Helgoland
Tel: 04725 800 0
Fax: 04725 800 444
ROOMS/FACILITIES: 51 rooms and suites, including 1 apartment
COMPLETION: 1999
CLIENT: Arne Weber
OPERATOR: Arne Weber
ARCHITECTURE: Alison Brooks Architects, NPS Architekten
Nietz, Prasch, Sigl
INTERIOR DESIGN: Alison Brooks Architects, Peter Andres

NAME: THE MERCER
ADDRESS: 147 Mercer Street
New York NY 10012
Tel: + 1 (212) 966 6060
Fax: + 1 (212) 965 3838
ROOMS/FACILITIES: 75 rooms; 5 suites; 'Mercer Kitchen'
restaurant; 'Cellar Lounge'
COMPLETION: 1998
CLIENT/OPERATOR: André Balazs
INTERIOR DESIGN: Christian Liaigre

NAME: THE RITZ-CARLTON
ADDRESS: StadtBrücke
38440 Wolfsburg
Tel: + 49 5361 60 7000
Fax: + 49 5361 60 8000
Web: www.ritzcarlton.com
ROOMS/FACILITIES: 174 rooms, including 19 Executive Suites, 34
Ritz-Carlton Club Rooms, 2 Ritz-Carlton Suites;
The Ritz-Carlton Club; 'Kraftwerk' health &
fitness centre; 2 restaurants: 'Aqua' (with
'Wine Lounge'), 'Vision'; private dining room;
'The Lobby Lounge' cocktail bar and tea room;
'Newman's' bar; meeting facilities
COMPLETION: 2000
CLIENT: Volkswagen
OPERATOR: The Ritz-Carlton Hotel Company of Germany
ARCHITECTURE: Dr. Günter Henn
INTERIOR DESIGN: Andrée Putman
SUBCONTRACTORS/SUPPLIERS: Wehberg, Eppinger, Schmidtke und Partner
(landscape design)

NAME:	BLAKES HOTEL
ADDRESS:	Keizersgracht 384
	1016 GB
	Amsterdam
	Tel: + 31 205 30 20 10
	Fax: + 31 205 30 20 30
ROOMS/FACILITIES:	26 rooms and 11 suites; 'Blakes' restaurant;
	'Long Gallery' restaurant; 'Blakes Bar';
	'Courtyard' restaurant; 'Annabel's' private
	dining room; meeting room
COMPLETION:	1998
CLIENT:	Anouska Hempel
OPERATOR:	Blakes
ARCHITECTURE & INTERIOR DESIGN:	Anouska Hempel

NAME:	KIRKETON HOTEL
ADDRESS:	229 Darlinghurst Road
	Darlinghurst
	Sydney NSW 2010
	Tel: 61 2 9332 2011
	Fax: 61 2 9332 2499
	E-mail: info@kirketon.com.au
	Web: www.kirketon.com.au
ROOMS/FACILITIES:	40 rooms; 'Salt' restaurant; 'Fix' bar; cocktail
	lounge; 'The Private Room'
	(conferences/private dining); nearby gym
COMPLETION:	1999
CLIENT:	Robert and Terry Schwamberg
OPERATOR:	Contemporary Hotels PLC
ARCHITECTURE & INTERIOR DESIGN:	Burley Katon Halliday
SUBCONTRACTORS/SUPPLIERS:	Fabio Ongarato Design (identity/graphic
	design)

NAME:	FITZWILLIAM HOTEL
ADDRESS:	St Stephen's Green
	Dublin 2
	Tel: +353 1 478 7000
	Fax: +353 1 478 7878
	Email: enq@fitzwilliam-hotel.com
ROOMS/FACILITIES:	130 rooms; 3 restaurant/bars: 'Peacock Alley',
	'Mango Toast', 'The Inn on the Green'; 3
	conference rooms
COMPLETION:	1998
CLIENT:	Fitzwilliam Hotel Group
OPERATOR:	Fitzwilliam Hotel Group
ARCHITECTURE:	Ashlin, Coleman, Heelan & O'Connor
INTERIOR DESIGN:	Conran & Partners
NAME:	GASTWERK HOTEL
ADDRESS:	Im "Forum Altes Gaswerk"
	Daimierstraße 67
	22761 Hamburg

	Tel: + 49 (0)40 890 62 0
	Fax: + 49 (0)40 890 62 20
	E-mail: info@gastwerk-hotel.de
	Web: www.gastwerk-hotel.de
ROOMS/FACILITIES:	90 rooms and 10 suites, including 1 Conran
	Suite; the 5 conference rooms; 6 team rooms;
	business lounge; 'Da Caio' restaurant; Winter
	Garden with Japanese restaurant; bar; Asiatic
	Relaxing Zone
COMPLETION:	1999
CLIENT:	Kai Hollman
OPERATOR:	Gastwerk Hotel Hamburg GmbH & Co KG
ARCHITECTURE & INTERIOR DESIGN:	Regine Schwethelm and Sybille Von Heyden

NAME:	FOUR SEASONS HOTEL CANARY RIVERSIDE
ADDRESS:	46 Westferry Circus
	Canary Wharf
	London E14 8RS
	Tel: + 44 (0)20 7510 1999
	Fax: + 44 (0)20 7510 1998
	Web: www.fourseasons.com/canarywharf
ROOMS/FACILITIES:	142 rooms and suites; Presidential Suite;
	'Quadrato' restaurant; 'Bar Quadrato'; fitness
	centre and health club
COMPLETION:	1999
CLIENT:	Four Seasons Hotels and Resorts
OPERATOR:	Four Seasons Hotels and Resorts
ARCHITECTURE & INTERIOR DESIGN:	United Designers Ltd., Renton Howard Wood
	Levin Partnership
SUBCONTRACTORS/SUPPLIERS:	John Sisk and Son Ltd. (main contractor)

NAME:	HOTEL HOPPER ST. ANTONIUS
ADDRESS:	Dagobertstraße 32
	50668 Cologne
	Tel: + 49 221 1660-0
	Fax: + 49 221 1660-166
	E-mail: st.antonius@hopper.de
ROOMS/FACILITIES:	39 rooms and 15 suites; conference centre;
	restaurant with garden; bar; sauna; solarium;
	fitness room; theatre
COMPLETION:	1999
CLIENT:	Hopper Hotels
OPERATOR:	Hopper Hotels
ARCHITECTURE & INTERIOR DESIGN:	HKR Architekten

NAME:	ONE ALDWYCH
ADDRESS:	1 Aldwych
	London WC2B 4BZ
	Tel: + 44 (0)20 7300 1000
	Fax: + 44 (0)20 7300 1001

ROOMS/FACILITIES: E-mail: sales@onealdwych.co.uk
Web: www.onealdwych.co.uk
ROOMS/FACILITIES: 105 rooms, including 12 suites; health club and pool; cinema; 'Axis' restaurant; 'Indigo' restaurant; lobby bar; 'The Cinammon Bar'; 3 meeting and private dining rooms
COMPLETION: 1998
CLIENT: Gordon Campbell Gray
OPERATOR: Dunraven Management Services
ARCHITECTURE: Jestico + Whiles + Associates
INTERIOR DESIGN: Jestico+ Whiles Interiors
SUBCONTRACTORS/SUPPLIERS: Gleeds (quantity surveyor); Cundall Johnston & Partners (structural and M+E consultants); Lighting Design International (lighting consultant); Hann Tucker (acoustic consultant).

NAME: GRAND HYATT BERLIN
ADDRESS: Marlene-Dietrich-Platz 2
10785 Berlin
Tel: + 49 30 2553 1234
Fax: + 49 30 2553 1235
Web: www.berlin.hyatt.com
ROOMS/FACILITIES: 342 rooms and suites, including two presidential suites; nine conference rooms; grand ballroom; 'Vox' restaurant with sushi bar; 'Tizian Italian Café'; 'Bistro Dietrich's';'Club Olympus' spa and fitness
COMPLETION: 1998
CLIENT: Hyatt International
OPERATOR: Hyatt International
ARCHITECTURE: José Rafael Moneo
INTERIOR DESIGN: Hannes Wettstein

NAME: DORINT DAS HOTEL AM GENDARMENMARKT
ADDRESS: Charlottenstraße 50-52
10117 Berlin
Tel: + 49 (0)30 20 27 5-0
Fax: + 49 (0)30 20 37 5-100
E-mail: info.Bergen@dorint.com
Web: www.dorint.de/berlin-gendarmenmarkt
ROOMS/FACILITIES: 92 rooms, including 22 suites
COMPLETION: 1999
CLIENT: Dorint AG
OPERATOR: DEFO
ARCHITECTURE & INTERIOR DESIGN: Harald Klein and Bert Haller, Mönchengladbach
SUBCONTRACTORS/SUPPLIERS: Abacus Architekten (main contractor); Ingenieurbüro Fritsch (electrical engineering)

NAME: THE ROGER WILLIAMS
ADDRESS: 131 Madison Avenue (at 31st St.)
New York
NY 10016
Tel: + 1 (212) 448 7000
Fax: + 1 (212) 448 7007
E-mail: rogerwilliams@boutiquehg.com
Web: www.rogerwilliamshotel.com
ROOMS/FACILITIES: 180 rooms; fitness studio; business centre
COMPLETION: 1997
CLIENT: The Gotham Hospitality Group
OPERATOR: Boutique Hotel Group
ARCHITECTURE & INTERIOR DESIGN: Rafael Viñoly Architects
MAIN CONTRACTOR: Vanguard Construction
SUBCONTRACTORS/SUPPLIERS: Severud Associates (structural engineering); DJM (interior contractor); Syska + Hennessy (lighting); Hill de Bernardo (designers); TSAO + CLS (lamps); RNA Mechanical Maintainence (plumbing contractor); Jamco Air Conditioning (mechanical contractor); QNCC Electric (electrical contractor); Rick Henschel Design (graphics)

NAME: GREAT EASTERN HOTEL
ADDRESS: Liverpool Street
London EC2M 7QN
Tel: + 44 (0)20 7618 5000
Fax: + 44 (0)20 7618 5001
E-mail: sales@great-eastern-hotel.co.uk
ROOMS/FACILITIES: 267 rooms, including 21 suites; gym; 4 restaurants: 'Aurora', 'Terminus', 'Miyabi', 'Fishmarket'; 3 bars; 12 private dining and event rooms; six-storey-high gallery, with glass roof and projection wall; 2 shops: 'Wild at Heart' florist', 'Ren' bath products
COMPLETION: 2000
CLIENT: Conran Holdings and Wyndham International
OPERATOR: Conran International
ARCHITECTURE: Manser Associates
INTERIOR & GRAPHIC DESIGN: Conran & Partners
SUBCONTRACTORS/SUPPLIERS: Jakobsen, Eames, van der Rohe, Conran & Partners (furniture)
Frette (bedlinen)

NAME: GRAND HYATT SHANGHAI
ADDRESS: Jin Mao Tower
88 Century Boulevard
Pudong
Shanghai 200121
People's Republic of China
Tel: + 86 21 5049 1234

ROOMS/FACILITIES: Fax: + 86 21 5049 1111
E-mail: info@hyattshanghai.com
555 rooms; 9 Business Suites; 17 executive
suites; 8 Regency Suites; 8 Diplomatic Suites;
2 Presidential Suites; 1 Chairman's Suite;
'Regency Club' (74 rooms; 8 suites; private
lounge; boardroom); communications centre;
beauty salon; clinic; shopping arcade; 12
restaurants and bars; 'Club Oasis' fitness
centre; swimming pool; 2 ballrooms; 7
function/drawing rooms, 2 conference rooms,
boardroom; exhibition hall and theatre

COMPLETION: 1999
CLIENT: China Shanghai Foreign Trade Centre Co. Ltd.
OPERATOR: Hyatt International Technical Systems
ARCHITECTURE & INTERIOR DESIGN: Skidmore, Owings & Merrill LLP (Chicago);
Bilkey Linas Design; Bregman & Hamann
Architects
SUBCONTRACTORS/SUPPLIERS: Shanghai Jin Mao (main contractor); Shen,
Milson & Wilke Ltd. (acoustical); Lerch, Bates
& Associates (exterior/interior maintenance);
Howard Field and Associates (fountain);
Woodward Clyde, Inc. (geotechnical); Edgett
Williams Consulting Group Inc. (vertical
transportation); Boundary Layer Wind Tunnel
Research Laboratory (wind engineering); Tino
Kwan Lighting Consultants (hotel lighting
consultants)

NAME: THE REGENT WALL STREET
ADDRESS: 55 Wall Street
New York NY 10005
Tel: + 1 (212) 845 8600
Fax: + 1 (212) 845 8601
Web: www.regenthotels.com
ROOMS/FACILITIES: 144 rooms, including 47 suites; 'Regent
Ballroom'; 11 meeting and function rooms; '55
Wall' restaurant; '55 Wall Terrace' restaurant
and bar; 'The Lounge'; 'Regent Spa'; business
centre
COMPLETION: 1999
CLIENT: Regent Hotels
OPERATOR: Regent Hotels
ARCHITECTURE & INTERIOR DESIGN: Wilson Associates, Michael Gadaleta Architects

NAME: PARK HYATT MELBOURNE
ADDRESS: 1 Parliament Square
Melbourne
Victoria 3002
Tel: 61 3 9224 1234
Fax: 61 3 9224 1200

ROOMS/FACILITIES: E-mail: phmelbourne@hyatt.com.au
241 rooms and suites; 'Park Club Health and
Day Spa'; business centre; 'Trilogy Bistro and
Lounge'; 'Radii' restaurant; 'Cuba' cigar lounge;
tea lounge; meeting and conference facilities;
'Regency Club'; ballroom
COMPLETION: 1999
CLIENT: Max Moar
OPERATOR: Hyatt Hotels
ARCHITECTURE & INTERIOR DESIGN: Tatron USA

NAME: THE GLENEAGLES HOTEL
ADDRESS: Auchterarder
Perthshire PH3 1NF
Scotland
Tel: (0)1764 662 231
Fax: (0)1764 662 134
Web: www.gleneagles.com
ROOMS/FACILITIES: 213 rooms and 13 suites; restaurants: 'The
Strathearn', 'Andrew Fairlie at Gleneagles', 'The
Club'; 'The Dormy Clubhouse'; 'The Bar';
conference and event facilities; golf; shooting;
riding; falconry; shops
COMPLETION: 1998
CLIENT: Guiness
OPERATOR: Guiness
ARCHITECTURE & INTERIOR DESIGN: Sedley Place
SUBCONTRACTORS/SUPPLIERS: A&L King (main contractor)

NAME: HOTEL KÄMP
ADDRESS: Pohjoisesplanadi 29
00100 Helsinki
Tel: + 358 (0)9 576 111
Fax: + 358 (0)9 576 1122
Web: www.courancove.com
ROOMS/FACILITIES: 179 Deluxe Rooms, including 6 Speciality
Suites and the Presidential Suite; 'Restaurant
Kämp'; 'CK's Brasserie'; 'The Bar and the
Library'; 'Terrace' restaurant; health club and
sauna; business centre; ballroom; 5
boardrooms; lobby shops
COMPLETION: 1999
CLIENT: Osakeyhtiö Kämp, Merita Real Estate
OPERATOR: Starwood Hotels & Resorts Worldwide Inc.
ARCHITECTURE & INTERIOR DESIGN: Julian Reed at EAA International

NAME: BURJ AL ARAB
ADDRESS: PO BOX 74147
Dubai
UAE

Tel: + 971-4-301 7777
Fax: + 971-4-301 7000
Web: www.burj-al-arab.com
ROOMS/FACILITIES: 202 suites; 7 restaurants and lounges; health club; business and conference facilities
COMPLETION: 1999
CLIENT: Jumeirah International
OPERATOR: Jumeirah International
ARCHITECTURE & INTERIOR DESIGN: WS Atkins; KCA International

NAME: COURAN COVE ISLAND RESORT
ADDRESS: South Stradbroke Island, Queensland, Australia
Tel: (91-141) 68 0101
Fax: (91-141) 68 0202
Web: www.courancove.com
ROOMS/FACILITIES: 357 rooms; restaurant; bars and cafés; sports centre; spa
COMPLETION: 1998
CLIENT: Inter Pacific Group
OPERATOR: Inter Pacific Group
ARCHITECTURE & INTERIOR DESIGN: Daryl Jackson Architects; Gilbert Gouveia (project architect)
SUBCONTRACTORS/SUPPLIERS: Sinclair Knight Merz (structural, civil and services consultant); Lincolne Scott (electrical and mechanical consultant); Funnell Hydraulics (hydraulics consultant); EDAW (landscape architect); Accent Lighting (lighting consultant); Watson Moss Growcott (acoustic consultant); Rider Hunt (quantity surveyor); Gibson Quai & Assocaites (communications consultant); Watpac (builder)

NAME: THE VENETIAN
ADDRESS: 3355 Las Vegas Boulevard South
Las Vegas NV 89109
Tel: + 1 (702) 733 5000
ROOMS/FACILITIES: 3036 suites; 5 swimming pools; spa; shopping mall; meetings and convention facility; casino; 16 restaurants
COMPLETION: 1999
OPERATOR: Las Vegas Sands Inc.
ARCHITECTURE: TSA of Nevada, LLP, WAT&G
INTERIOR DESIGN: Dougall Design and Wilson & Associates

NAME: PARIS
ADDRESS: 3655 Las Vegas Boulevard
South Las Vegas
Las Vegas NV 89109
Tel: + 1 (702) 946 7000

Web: www.parislasvegas.com
ROOMS/FACILITIES: 2916 rooms, including 295 suites; spa; pool; ballroom; casino; 10 restaurants; theatre; 6 lounges; business centre
COMPLETION: 1999
CLIENT: Park Place Entertainment Corporation
OPERATOR: Park Place Entertainment Corporation
ARCHITECTURE: Bergman, Walls & Youngblood Ltd.,
INTERIOR DESIGN: Yates-Silverman, Inc., Kovacs & Associates

NAME: SHERATON MIRAMAR RESORT HOTEL
ADDRESS: El Gouna
Red Sea
Egypt
Tel: 20 65 545606
Fax: 20 65 545608
Web: www.sheraton.com
ROOMS/FACILITIES: 250 rooms; 2 restaurants with bars; pool
COMPLETION: 1997
CLIENT: Orascom Tourist Establishments
OPERATOR: Sheraton Corporation
ARCHITECTURE: Michael Graves Architects, Rami El Dahan & Soheir Fahid Architects
INTERIOR DESIGN: Michael Graves Architects and Ibrahim Nagi
SUBCONTRACTORS/SUPPLIERS: Hydroscapes Egypt (landscape architect); Hamza Associates (landscape architect); Bakry Engineers (engineering consultants)

NAME: HOUSE OF BLUES HOTEL
ADDRESS: 333 North Dearborn Street
Chicago IL 60610
Tel: + 1 (312) 245 0333
Fax: + 1 (312) 923 2458
Web: www.loewshotels.com
ROOMS/FACILITIES: 367 rooms, including 12 Junior, 3 Grand and 7 VIP suites; meeting facilities; 'House of Blues' restaurant; 'Smith & Wollensky's New York Steak and Chop House'; 'CRUNCH' health centre and spa; bowling; 'Kaz Bar'
COMPLETION: 1998
CLIENT: LOEWS
OPERATOR: LOEWS
ARCHITECTURE & INTERIOR DESIGN: Cheryl Rowley

NAME: ATLANTIS
ADDRESS: Paradise Island
Nassau
Bahamas
Tel: 242-363 -3000
Fax: 242-363-6309

ROOMS/FACILITIES: Web: www.atlantis.com
2325 rooms; 18 restaurants; Grand Ballroom;
20 lounges and clubs; casino; sports centre;
spa; golf
COMPLETION: 1998
CLIENT: Sun International
OPERATOR: Sun International
ARCHITECTURE & INTERIOR DESIGN: Wimberly, Allison, Tong & Goo

NAME: MIRACLE MANOR RETREAT
ADDRESS: 12589 Reposa Way
Desert Hot Springs
California 92240
Tel: 760 329 6641
Fax: (0)30 20 37 5-100
Web: www.miraclemanor.com
ROOMS/FACILITIES: 6 rooms; swimming pool and hot tub; spa
COMPLETION: continually evolving
CLIENT: April Greiman and Michael Rotondi
OPERATOR: April Greiman and Michael Rotondi
ARCHITECTURE & INTERIOR DESIGN: April Greiman and Michael Rotondi

NAME: RAJVILÂS
ADDRESS: Goner Road
Jaipur 303 012
India
Tel: (91-141) 68 0101
Fax: (91-141) 68 0202
E-mail: reservations@rajvilas.com
Web: www.oberoihotels.com
ROOMS/FACILITIES: 54 Deluxe Rooms; 13 Luxury Tents; 'Royal
Villa'; 'Surya Mahal' restaurant; pool bar;
'Rajwada' library bar; 'Tijori' boutique; spa; pool;
2 tennis courts;
COMPLETION: 1998
CLIENT: Oberoi Hotels
OPERATOR: Oberoi Hotels
ARCHITECTURE & INTERIOR DESIGN: Prabhat Patki, H.L Lim & Associates
SUBCONTRACTORS/SUPPLIERS: Bill Bensley (landscape architect)

NAME: POUSADA SANTA MARIA DO BOURO
ADDRESS: 4720-688 AMARES
Tel: 253 37 19 71/2/3
Fax: 253 37 19 76
E-mail: guest@pousadas.pt
Web: www.pousadas.pt
ROOMS/FACILITIES: 30 rooms and 2 suites; meeting facilities;
restaurant; pool; tennis court; fishing
COMPLETION: 1997
CLIENT: ENATUR

OPERATOR: Pousadas de Portugal
ARCHITECTURE & INTERIOR DESIGN: Eduardo Souto do Mouro, Cecilia Cavaca,
Humerto Vieira
SUBCONTRACTORS/SUPPLIERS: GOP, Porto (structural and electrical engineer)

NAME: NGORONGORO CRATER LODGE
ADDRESS: Ngorongoro
Tanzania
Tel: + 27 11 809 4300
Fax: + 27 11 809 4400
Web: www.ccafrica.com
ROOMS/FACILITIES: 30 suites in 3 camps; dining room in each
camp
COMPLETION: 1997
OPERATOR: CC Africa
ARCHITECTURE & INTERIOR DESIGN: Silvio Rech, Lesley Carstens, Chris Browne
SUBCONTRACTORS/SUPPLIERS: Work carried out by local artisans

NAME: HOTEL MADLEIN
ADDRESS: 6165 Ischgl, Austria
Tel: + 43(0) 5444/5226
Fax: + 43 (0) 5444/5226 202
Web: www.ischglmadlein.com
ROOMS/FACILITIES: 80 rooms; restaurant and 'Wunderbar'; 'Fire
Room', with open fireplace; Zen garden; indoor
pool; gym; sauna; beauty spa
COMPLETION: 2000
CLIENT: Günther Aloys
OPERATOR: Büro Burgstaller
ARCHITECTURE & INTERIOR DESIGN: Mescherowsky Architekten
SUBCONTRACTORS/SUPPLIERS: Fa. Kreidl (heating/ventilation/sanitaryware);
Dr Rupp (architectural psychologist); Gehrer,
Bregenz (stress analyst); Fa. Revoluce
(lighting analyst); Obex-Pfeifer (surveyor)

NAME: DEVI GARH
ADDRESS: PO BOX No 144
Udaipur 313001
Rajasthan
Tel: 91 2953-89211
Fax: 91 2953-89357
E-mail: reservations@deviresorts.com
ROOMS/FACILITIES: 23 suites and 6 tents; restaurant; bar;
conference and banqueting facilities; library;
fitness centre; spa; pool; beauty parlour;
shopping arcade
COMPLETION: 1999
CLIENT: Devi Resorts
OPERATOR: Heritage Hotels
ARCHITECTURE & INTERIOR DESIGN: Rajiv Saini & Associates

NAME:	PALAU SA FONT
ADDRESS:	C.\ Apuntadores 38
	E-07012 Palma de Mallorca
	Balleares
	Tel: + 34 971 712 277
	Fax: + 34 971 712 618
	E-mail: info@palausafont.com
ROOMS/FACILITIES:	15 rooms and 4 suites; pool; bar; meeting facilities
COMPLETION:	2000
CLIENT:	Ricarda Söhnlein, Tom Gösmann
ARCHITECTURE:	Andreu Bennassar
INTERIOR DESIGN:	Hans-Jürgen Pahl

NAME:	EXPLORA EN ATACAMA
ADDRESS:	San Pedro de Atacama
	Northern Chile
	Tel: (Santiago office: 56-2/206-6060)
	Fax: (Santiago office: 56-2/228-4655)
ROOMS/FACILITIES:	50 rooms with jacuzzi; meeting/music room; 4 outdoor pools; 4 saunas; stables
COMPLETION:	1998
CLIENT:	Explora
OPERATOR:	Explora
A RCHITECTURE & INTERIOR DESIGN:	Germán de Sol
SUBCONTRACTORS/SUPPLIERS:	Horacio Schmidt, Nicole Labbé, Hernán Fierro, Carlos Venegas (project team); Fernando de Sol (structural engineer); Francisco Cervantes (services engineer); Renato Lorca (services engineer)

NAME:	ANASSA HOTEL
ADDRESS:	Latsi
	8840 Polis
	Cyprus
	Tel: + 357 6 888 000
	Fax: + 357 6 322 900
	E-mail: anassa@thanos-hotels.com.cy
ROOMS/FACILITIES:	186 rooms and suites, with terrace or balcony; 2 outdoor pools; 1 indoor pool; water sports; tennis; gym; games facilities; spa; 4 restaurants; bars and cafés; boutique; banqueting and conference facilities.
COMPLETION:	1998
CLIENT:	Thanos Hotels Ltd.
OPERATOR:	Thanos Hotels Ltd.
ARCHITECTURE:	Sandy & Babcock
INTERIOR DESIGN:	James Northcutt Associates; Darrel Schmitt Design Associate
SUBCONTRACTORS/SUPPLIERS:	Ecoplan (landscape design); Alecos Gabrielides (Local Architect)

NAME:	FOUR SEASONS RESORT AT SAYAN
ADDRESS:	Sayan
	Ubud
	Gianyar 80571
	Bali
	Tel: (62-361) 977 577
	Fax: (62-361) 977 588
	Web: www.fourseasons.com
ROOMS/FACILITIES:	18 suites; 28 villas with private plunge pools; 2 restaurants; 'Jati Bar'; library and lounge; exercise room and Indonesian spa; pool; gallery and boutique
COMPLETION:	1998
CLIENT:	Four Seasons Hotels and Resorts
OPERATOR:	Four Seasons Hotels and Resorts
ARCHITECTURE & INTERIOR DESIGN:	Heah & Co.
SUBCONTRACTORS/SUPPLIERS:	Site Concepts International, Singapore & Estetika Karya (landscape design)

NAME:	CASA TEGOYA
ADDRESS:	Calle Conil-Asomada Nr. 3
	35572 Conil
	Lanzarote
	Tel: + 34 928 834385
	Fax: + 34 928 834369
	www.casategoyo.com
FACILITIES:	12 rooms; à la carte restaurant; bar; patio; sun terrace; 2 pools; conference room
COMPLETION:	1999
OWNER/OPERATOR:	Heidi Hupe
ARCHITECT & INTERIOR DESIGNER:	Heidi Hupe

NAME:	ICEHOTEL
ADDRESS:	981 91 Jukkasjärvi
	Sweden
	Tel: + 46 (0)980 66 800
	Fax: + 46 (0)980 66 890
	Email: info@icehotel.com
	Web: www.icehotel.com
ROOMS/FACILITIES:	6 igloos; 30 cabins; 'Aurora' houses; 'Absolut Bar'; art centre; 'Jukkasjärvi Wärdshus'; 'Jukkasjärvi Village'; 'Ice Church'; conference facilities
COMPLETION:	December each year
CLIENT:	ICEHOTEL AB
OPERATOR:	Jukkas AB
ARCHITECTURE & INTERIOR DESIGN:	Åke Larsson

Photographic credits

The author and the publishers would like to thank the designers and architects involved in the creation of this book and the following photographers and copyright holders for the use of their material. We apologize for any possible omission from this list.

Jaime Ardiles (136–139); Daniel Aubry (158–161); Bally's & Paris Photography (154–157); Courtesy of Brighter PR (122–125); Richard Bryant/ARCAID (181); Chris Caldicott (178–180); Mike Caldwell (132–135); David Cantwell (78–81); Dook Clunies-Ross (186–189); Peter Cook/VIEW (112–115); Courtesy of Couran Cove Island Resort (146–149); Rolant Dafis/ARCAID (28 right, 30–31); Todd Eberle (20–21, 28 left, 60, 61 left); Damir Fabijanic (34–35); Annette Fischer (36–37); Andrea Flak (82–85); Four Seasons Hotels and Resorts (86–88, 212); Klaus Frahm/artur (23–27); Jeff Goldberg/ESTO (109); Courtesy of Grand Hyatt Shanghai (117–121); Courtesy of Hyatt International (126); Tim Griffith (127–131); Eberhard Hahne (200–203); Roland Halbe/artur (98–101); Rio Helmi (212–217); Courtesy Anouska Hempel (67–71); Jorg Hempel (218–221); Daniel Infanger (53, 56 bottom); Jan Jordan (222–227); Courtesy Jumeirah International (141–144); Nicholas Kane/ARCAID (29, 32–33); Christophe Kicherer (54, 56 top, 57); Ken Kirkwood (96); Michael Kleinberg (108, 110–111); John Lodge (175, 176 bottom, 177); Duccio Malagamba (182–185); Veits Muller/artur (52, 54 bottom); Michael Mundy (45–46, 59, 61 right); Nacasa & Partners (48–51); Henri del Olmo (208–211) Courtesy One Aldwych (94, 97); Amit Pashricha (194–199); Courtesy of Pentagram (173,174); Red Cover/Ken Hayden (89); Red Cover/James Mitchell (95); Sharrin Rees (72–77); Philippe Ruault (13–17); Soenne (102–107, 190–193); Courtesy Sun International (150–153, 166, 168–171 top); Tim Street-Porter (2, 38–43); Peter Vitale (167, 171 bottom); Morley Von Sternberg/ARCAID (18–19); Simon Watson (58); Guy Wemborne (204–207)

index